Educating Drug-Exposed Children

Educating Drug-Exposed Children

*The Aftermath
of the Crack-Baby Crisis*

Janet Y. Thomas

ROUTLEDGEFALMER
NEW YORK AND LONDON

Published in 2004 by
RoutledgeFalmer
29 West 35th Street
New York, New York 10001
www.routledgefalmer.com

Published in Great Britain by
RoutledgeFalmer
11 New Fetter Lane
London EC4P 4EE
www.routledge.co.uk

RoutledgeFalmer is an imprint of the Taylor & Francis Group.

Printed in the United States of America on acid-free paper.

10 9 8 7 6 5 4 3 2 1

Library of Congress Cataloging-in-Publication Data

Thomas, Janet Y., 1968-
  Educating drug-exposed children : the aftermath of the crack baby crisis / Janet Y. Thomas.
    p. cm.
  Includes bibliographical references and index.
  ISBN 0-415-94893-2 (alk. paper)—ISBN 0-415-94894-0 (pbk. : alk. paper)
  1. Children of prenatal substance abuse—Education—United States. I. Title.
  LC4806.4.T56 2004
  371.92—dc22

                                                                    2003069773

Contents

Acknowledgments

This book could not have been completed without the support of my family, friends, mentors, and colleagues. I would like to take time to thank every one of you for giving me what was needed to start, work through, and complete this task. First and foremost, I would like to thank my parents, Mrs. Florence Rose Thomas and the late Enoch Thomas Sr., for teaching me the value of higher education, and my twin sister, Janice Y. Thomas, who has supported me the longest and the strongest. A special thank-you is also extended to my aunt, Frances C. Robinson, for your unconditional support, and to other family members—you know who you are.

My senior mentors deserve an honorable mention. Without your guidance, constructive criticism, encouragement, and reviews of this manuscript, *Educating Drug-Exposed Children* would have never become a reality. A special acknowledgment is extended to Dr. Sam Stringfield, my mentor at Johns Hopkins. I will be forever grateful to Sam. You have provided the time, the space, and the encouragement necessary for me to complete this project. Dr. Larry Parker, at the University of Illinois at Urbana-Champaign in the Department of Educational Policy Studies, has had an equal influence on this work. Without your guidance, this idea would have never become a reality. You have taught me the value of educational policy studies in the context of at-risk students and given me the courage to pursue such a hot topic. I would also like to thank Dr. James Anderson, Dr. Wanda Pillow, Dr. Bill Trent, and Dr. Kal Alston in the Department of Educational Policy Studies at the University of Illinois. A special acknowledgment is also extended to Dr. Kathy Ryan in the Department of Educational Psychology, also at the University of Illinois.

I would also like to give a special thank-you to Dr. Wendy G. Winters, Howard University, Center for Education of Students Placed at Risk. I really appreciated your guidance, words of wisdom, support, and friendship during the tough times. I would also like to send a special thank you to Dr. Meg Meguire at Kings College, University of London, for encouraging me to write more about this topic; to Dr. Pedro A. Noguera at New York University's Steinhardt School of Education for your comments and suggestions on the first rough draft; to Diane Powell, former Director of Project DAISY program for drug-exposed children in Washington, D.C.; and to Ms. Carien Williams for lending me your good editorial eye.

A special thanks is also extended to the teacher participants: Gloria, Brenda, Jeanne, Stephanie, Troy, Eleanor, Angela, Peggy, Ms. De'Ella, and Bernie.

Foreword

Educational policy has become a bureaucratic instrument with which to administer the expectations that the public has for education. The language of educational policy has served to establish public agenda issues with the development of new policies. However, this language has also been used to exclude certain issues from the arena of public debate or resist certain claims made by various interest groups.[1] The critical educational policy analysis perspective stems from the work of Michelle Young, Jim Scheurich, Steven Ball, and others who have essentially engaged in a type of policy tracing (e.g., genealogy, archeology) that asks the fundamental question of how politics and policy development, formulation, implementation, and evaluation have multiple and conflicting impacts on various populations, particularly those the policy is intended to serve.[2]

Janet Thomas's work builds on this perspective of critical educational policy analysis by looking at how the battle lines over drug intervention policy overlapped with educational policy issues during the late 1980s and early 1990s. This work discusses the struggle for educational policies and programs for children impacted by the urban drug crisis. In addition to the policy discussions, the text presents the voices of teachers who are working with drug-impacted children who are now in elementary school or special education settings. The teachers neither demonize the children nor paint a portrait of model students. Rather, the teacher interviews reveal the complexity of working with these students, and show how their learning needs, their goals, and their parents' desires are similar to those of students in regular classrooms. This is important in that the teachers of these students often have been the missing voice in the policy discourse on crack cocaine's impact on urban schooling.

Equally important are the policy recommendations that flow from the teacher interviews. If policy makers mean what they say about "leaving no child behind," they would take seriously the specific remedies suggested in this book for these particular drug-impacted children. For example, even though most of the medical literature cites no differences between drug-exposed children and other students, teachers explain how the former group is more vulnerable to early school failure. Therefore, it is imperative that steps be taken to change the classroom climate and teaching and learning expectations to ensure more positive learning experiences for these students. To be sure, the demonstration projects started in the early 1990s with preschool-age drug-exposed children were successful. However, these initiatives were not continued into the public school arena. From a policy implementation standpoint, the success of the preschool projects needs to be tested in the public schools in a more systematic way, with the programs adapted to the specific needs of these older children. A major policy implication is the suggested changes in teacher preparation to deal with this population, as well as curriculum and instructional changes. The policy implications and recommendations noted by the author are particularly important for special educators in that school officials should not be so quick to label students who are from drug-impacted families. Instead, they should work with these families and with social service providers to create a better transition to elementary school and increase the opportunities for this particular set of children to remain in regular classes.

Dr. Thomas's work attempts to get readers to engage in some critical thinking about the legacy of the crack epidemic and its real and perceived impact on urban education. Some of the critical questions that she wants readers to look at through her book are: How did the crack epidemic get defined? What were the resulting laws and policies that stemmed from media reporting of the crack baby crisis and political action by lawmakers? What was the major underlying bias of the research that framed the minority drug problem, particularly as it affected low-socioeconomic-status African-American and Latina women and their children? How have administrators and teachers in schools bought into this ideology of crack use and its effect on children? What assumptions are made with these students? Will they continue to be profiled as problem children who belong in special education or alternative settings? The questions that Dr. Thomas raises in this book have important policy implications that need to be interjected into the debate concerning whether educators, administrators, social workers, psychologists, evaluators, lawyers, judges, and the general public are seriously addressing the needs of drug-exposed children.

Janet Thomas has written a book of critical importance for social policy and education policy regarding a group of students to which society has done a disservice. She does not necessarily provide answers for teachers, administrators, and others connected to the education of this population; rather, she has more to say about the ideology of educational policy, what is said and what is left out of educational policy discourse, and whom it affects in multiple and conflicting ways. I was Janet's advisor when she was a doctoral student at the University of Illinois at Urbana-Champaign. She took key classes from all of us here in the department in which she developed her depth of understanding of critical educational policy analysis. After completing her doctoral work here, she has gone on to great achievements at Johns Hopkins as a researcher and scholar who has proven herself at many levels. As an advisor, I always hope that my students will go on to do even better than I have done, and this is what I see Janet doing with this book. I am honored to have worked with her and expect that she will continue to engage in critical studies of educational policy issues that have an effect on urban education.

Laurence Parker
July 2002

Introduction

In 1990 the United States Department of Health and Human Services, Office of the Inspector General, released its first report on the number of children being born prenatally exposed to drugs, entitled *Crack Babies*.[1] Although the escalating number of cases of drug-exposed infants was already a concern, this document highlighted the growing rate among poor urban women and the need to put more direct effort into addressing the problem. This widely cited report estimated that 375,000 drug-exposed infants were born during the 1980s and predicted that the number of births would total nearly 4 million by the year 2000.[2] These children became known as the crack generation—children born to poor urban drug-abusing women. Crack babies were believed to be a growing biological underclass; they were portrayed as severely neurologically damaged and beyond rehabilitation. Public policy experts predicted that crack babies would use up available human services resources, dominate health care facilities, and consume most of the special education resources; immediate policy interventions were needed to address the problem.

Since the mid-1980s, drug-exposed children have been at the heart of social, public health, and educational policy discussions. These children have been researched and written about more extensively than any other group of substance-exposed children. Interest in their drug-related impairments became the focus of policy discussions in the context of the ongoing drug problem and efforts to address prenatal substance abuse. However, social construction of the urban drug epidemic stigmatized crack-abusing women and their children, ultimately criminalizing prenatal substance abuse. Crack mothers and their prenatally exposed children attracted national attention until around 1994, when the topic vanished from the mainstream media. The developmental adversities of crack-exposed babies were no longer the major issue. Their developmental needs became lost in larger public policy discussions regarding how to best address drug abuse among the American socially and economically disadvantaged. Support for the developmental challenges of drug-impacted children has received the least attention in the governmental response to the ongoing drug problem.

Drug-impacted children have truly become a lost generation. As you will read, their educational struggles have been exploited and neglected and are no longer seen as issues for policy makers or public schools to address. Despite the early stereotypes about the potential of drug-exposed children, later research gave educators a reason for optimism about the developmental expectations for drug-impacted children. Studies demonstrated that although prenatal drug exposure does cause some developmental deficiencies, these children are not biologically inferior, and with the appropriate interventions many can overcome their challenges.

So, how are schools responding to this population? This book answers this question and gives the first public school perspective on this issue. It draws attention back to the importance of responding to the needs of drug-affected children, as these youngsters have been displaced in the educational policy literature regarding at-risk schoolchildren and developmental challenges. Most importantly, it points out that if public education wishes to more effectively prevent early school failure, it must begin to acknowledge and intervene on behalf of this population. This story challenges educational policy makers to respond to the needs of all vulnerable children in U.S. public schools, thus supporting the commitment behind the slogan "No Child Left Behind."

Both my professional experiences and my scholarly training have shaped my passion for this topic. In addition to my background in educational policy formation and implementation and the politics of the policy process, I have almost ten years of experience as a practitioner in the human services profession. During this time, I served as a therapeutic social worker, psychotherapist, and case manager for drug-impacted families with high-risk children. This has allowed me to develop a comprehensive understanding of the problem, which has influenced the scope of this work. Although educational policy is the primary focus, the content and scope speak to a wide audience. The policy and intervention recommendations have implications for health and human service professionals, early intervention providers, and family-focused drug-treatment programs, as well as educational policy makers.

Divided into two main sections, the text is organized to provide a comprehensive understanding of the urban crack baby crisis and the issues involved with educating drug-impacted children. The first half, "Poor Urban Drug-Abusing Women and Crack Babies," discusses the influences on policy solutions designed to respond to the problem of drug-impacted families with dependent children. This section gives special attention to the social construction of the urban crack baby crisis and its influence on expectations for drug-exposed children. It also explains how clinical opinion regarding the effects of prenatal drug exposure altered during various periods during the 1990s, which contributed to the difficulties of defining drug-impacted children in the context of educational policy.

The second half, "Educating Drug-Exposed Children," provides a public school perspective on the educational experiences of drug-exposed children with developmental challenges. Focusing specifically on the school-age population, this section provides insights into their educational difficulties and explains why, despite their capabilities, these children are extremely vulnerable to early school failure. Most importantly, this section examines public school perceptions of children who were prenatally exposed to drugs and demonstrates the need for a knowledge base on the school-age population. This portion of the book points out that the troubles with educating drug-exposed schoolchildren are not caused by the nature of their impairments. Rather, the problem lies in the fact that public education is not prepared to meet their specific needs.

While this volume focuses on the educational struggles of children prenatally exposed to drugs, it also raises broader questions about how public schools are addressing the needs of young children with developmental delays in general. It critically examines special education programs and the practice of full inclusion as they relate to children with nontraditional disabilities, such as drug-exposed children, in public school systems with limited resources. Most importantly, this work points out the need to give more attention to young children with correctable developmental delays, as they are often inappropriately placed in special education settings with children with more serious developmental disabilities.

Taken together, the individual chapters provide a comprehensive understanding of the social and educational policy conflicts affecting drug-exposed children and their families. Following this introduction, Chapter 1, "The Policy Paradox," traces the historical development of the crack baby crisis and discusses the influence of political ideology and media images in framing prenatal substance abuse during the 1980s. Giving specific attention to crack-abusing mothers, it specifically demonstrates how public reactions to these women were embedded in the race and class politics, and how policies to address the problem were formulated accordingly. Specifically, the chapter examines how prenatal substance abuse among poor urban women was depicted as a moral disease and a criminal pathology, both of which help justify punitive social policies. The challenges that drug-affected families presented to the social welfare system during the crack era and the prevailing public policy conflicts are also discussed.

Chapter 2, "Drug-Exposed Children and Development," reviews the medical research concerning the developmental implications of prenatal drug exposure. Beginning with the 1980s, the chapter outlines the literature on children who became known as "crack babies" during the late 1980s and early 1990s and discusses the research on their developmental outcomes. The debate about "crack baby syndrome" is also detailed in the context of misconceptions about the impact of drug exposure and the challenges of researching this topic. This chapter also demonstrates how the lack of consensus regarding the impact of drug exposure inadvertently hindered educational policy efforts and contributed to the lack of attention given to the school-age population.

Chapter 3, "The Politics of At-Risk," discusses educational policy decisions during the 1990s in regard to the early-intervention needs of at-risk children, particularly drug-impacted children, with particular attention given to the amendments made to special education policy, specifically those for children with nonconventional disabilities. The drug-exposed population is examined in terms of how it did or did not benefit from the infant and toddler programs and special education preschool programs developed under the Individuals with Disabilities in Education Act (IDEA).

Chapter 4, "Identifying a Cracked Foundation," includes information from interviews gathered from public-school teachers in Champaign, Illinois; Cook County, Illinois; and Baltimore, Maryland, regarding the school experiences of drug-impacted children and the need for education-oriented interventions. How public schools have responded to these children is the focus of this chapter. Teachers discuss the children's developmental difficulties, the psychosocial risk factors, and the special education dilemma. Their insights help provide a better understanding of the struggles that drug-exposed schoolchildren endure. The challenges of working with these children in general education settings that are not designed to meet their needs are also discussed.

The final chapter, "Healing the Crack in Their World," places the developmental needs of drug-impacted children into the discussion on drug policy, particularly as it relates to prenatal substance abuse. This section explains why addressing the needs of drug-exposed children must take an integrated approach that includes professionals in the areas of public health, early intervention, family-focused drug treatment programs, and education—most importantly, the public school. Challenging education professionals to "expand the knowledge base," the chapter offers suggestions for improving the school experiences of drug-impacted children and the early interventions targeted at them.

PART I

Poor Urban Drug-Abusing Women and Crack Babies: The Making of an Epidemic

Need is also a political instrument,
meticulously prepared, calculated, and used.
—Michel Foucault

CHAPTER 1

The Policy Paradox
Responding to Prenatal Drug Abuse

Introduction

Since the mid-1980s, U.S. policy makers have been discussing how best to address the needs of families impacted by drug abuse. Parental substance abuse was no new phenomenon to child welfare services. However, crack-impacted families have nonconventional needs that represented new challenges to human services professionals. Drug treatment programs had the responsibility of responding to the needs of crack-abusing mothers, many of whom were pregnant; the health care community was uncertain about how prenatal drug exposure would affect babies; and existing social service agencies lacked the knowledge and resources to effectively intervene. As a result, many new social policies and programs were initiated.

The way in which a problem is defined dictates the established policy interventions. Prenatal substance abuse among poor urban women is a controversial issue and resulted in two contrasting policy objectives. First, there was a politicized interpretation that focused exclusively on the transgressions of crack-abusing mothers. This punitive approach prevailed throughout the late 1980s and early 1990s. Toward the end of the 1990s policy solutions turned toward more therapeutic solutions. This focus called for better social service interventions and gender-specific drug treatment programs. However, societal animosity toward poor drug-abusing mothers remained an underlying influence on policy solutions. Such paradoxes in problem definition are essentially struggles to define needs, and as scholars have long argued, "the interpretation of people's needs is itself a political stake."[1]

How were the needs of poor crack-abusing women and their babies defined by U.S. politicians and policy makers during the 1980s? What is the difference between pregnant women defined as "coke-using" and those characterized as "crack-abusing"? What types of human services policies are better suited for drug-impacted families involving dependent children? How should drug treatment programs respond to pregnant women or mothers with children? Should prenatal substance abuse be considered a child abuse issue or a medical condition that needs to be treated?

The above questions are examined in the context of forces that helped define prenatal substance abuse during the inception of the crack cocaine era. Such issues are also analyzed in terms of media-created images of pregnant drug-abusing women, public sentiment toward poor mothers on AFDC, and the social and political trends of the 1980s, which ultimately influenced a social construction of crack-abusing mothers and their infants. This chapter is essential to understanding how many social policies implemented to protect drug-affected babies were not designed in their best interest. It explains how, although there was much focus on projected outcomes for these children, not much attention has been given to the long-term effects of prenatal drug exposure. As a result, not enough effort has been put into addressing their specific developmental needs at the educational policy level.

Crack Cocaine, the Media, and the Public: The Social and Political Construction of the Urban Crack Baby Crisis

The news media served as a powerful political tool during the American drug epidemic of the 1980s, negatively impacting public perceptions of drug abusers. The media's drug narratives juxtaposed race and class politics, which influenced disparities in governmental responses to "coke users" and "crack abusers." Although cocaine use reached its peak in the mid-1970s, media coverage began during the 1980s and can be divided into two phases.

During the first phase, 1981–1985, coverage featured drug abusers who were White and middle-class, who sniffed cocaine for recreational purposes.[2] In these stories, the drug was portrayed as upscale and glamorous, earning nicknames such as the "champagne of drugs," "schoolboy," and "the rich man's drug." Public service announcements primarily advocated better treatment programs for Americans addicted to cocaine. Such themes suggested that the drug, not the drug abusers, was the root of the problem.

During this phase, rehabilitation was promoted as the ideal intervention for women who used drugs while pregnant. Coke-snorting women were portrayed as remorseful and concerned about the possible adverse effects of cocaine abuse on their newborns. The morality of expecting mothers using harmful substances was not a major focus.

For example, in September 1985 the first results of a study showing that pregnant women who used cocaine were more likely to miscarry was the topic of a major news report.[3] Featuring a White woman who admitted to using cocaine while expecting, the public health announcement cautioned about the effects of prenatal drug exposure, stating "The Message Is Clear, If You Are Pregnant and Use Cocaine—Stop."[4] These "soft" warnings can be found in most early discussions of cocaine use during pregnancy.

Media images shifted during the second phase, 1985–1986, when cocaine trickled down into low-income and working-class communities.[5] During this transformation, news reports focused on how inner-city neighborhoods were being torn apart by crack—a new, inexpensive, and smokable form of cocaine. Such stories introduced a new drug subculture of crack addicts, crack houses, crack dealers, crack mothers, and crack babies to the American public. For instance, CBS aired a captivating documentary called *48 Hours on a Crack Street,* which detailed the horrors of the urban crack world.[6] In competition, NBC ran a special entitled *Cocaine Country,* Making the crack-cocaine culture more compelling, by mid 1986 Newsweek Magazine called crack the biggest story since Watergate and Vietnam, and Time Magazine featured the urban crack story in the magazine's "Issue of the Year." "suggested that cocaine and crack use had become pandemic."[7] Contrasting with rehabilitation suggestions for coke users, stronger law enforcement and stiffer sentences for drug-related offenses were portrayed as the answer to the cocaine problem in inner-city neighborhoods.

Urban drug war stories set the context for the subsequent narratives of crack mothers and crack babies. As with the overall image of the crack problem, race and socioeconomic status influenced the journalistic portrayal of pregnant drug-abusing women. These images contributed to the social construction of prenatal substance abuse as a problem of poor urban minority women.

Narratives about crack-abusing pregnant inner-city women depicted them as lacking maternal instincts and caring only about supporting their addiction. According to news reports, their crack-exposed babies were permanently damaged—part of a growing biological underclass.[8] The underlying messages shifted to the defective characters of drug-abusing mothers and the adverse outcomes of their babies—"babies who, according to [one] reporter were 'victims who aren't even old enough to know better.' "[9] Newspaper articles carried headlines such as "For Pregnant Addict, Crack Comes First," "Babies: The Worst Threat Is Mom Herself," and "Crack's

Tiniest and Costliest Victims."[10] Reeves and Campbell concluded in *Crack Coverage: Television, News, the Anti-Drug Crusade and the Reagan Era:*

> Such journalistic horror stories that cast the mother in the role of the monster would take on racial overtones in 1986. In keeping with the general paradigm shift in the framing of drug news, the "cocaine mothers" of the 1985 warnings were predominantly white, and the "crack mothers" of the coverage in 1986–88 were predominantly women of color. In this shift, the discourse of the crack mother would resonate with the "cultural Moynihamism" of the "new racism"—the "epidemic" of crack babies became yet another example of the "poverty of values" crippling America's black inner cities.

Reeves and Campbell found such dichotomous imagery parallel to what Rickie Solinger sketched in her study of single women, pregnancy, and race prior to *Roe v. Wade*.[12] Solinger uncovered similar biases in responses to the rising rates of illegitimate children at midcentury. Single White women who became pregnant were portrayed as offenders, which motivated social service agencies to redefine illegitimacy. Consequently, unwed motherhood for White women came to be viewed "as a psychological rather than a sexual issue," and intervention was introduced in the context of social work services.[13] In contrast, single Black women who became pregnant were constructed as delinquents; their pregnancy was defined according to their "uncontrolled sexual indulgence" and "absence of psyche"—these women had "no personality structure."[14] Reeves and Campbell found "the same black/white, therapy/pathology, recovery/discrimination, inclusion/exclusion" distinctions in the drug baby narratives of the 1980s.[15]

Despite popular assumptions regarding race, class, and prenatal substance abuse, research demonstrates that poor minority women are no more likely to use drugs during pregnancy than White middle-class women.[16] A National Institute on Drug Abuse survey gathered self-reported data from a national sample of women in fifty-two rural and urban hospitals. The study noted that African-American women had the highest rates of crack use. However, White women reported overall higher rates of substance abuse during pregnancy. The study reported that an estimated number of women who used drugs while pregnant, and 113,000 were White, 75,000 were African-American, and 28,000 were Hispanic.[17]

Political and Cultural Issues:
Crack Mothers, Welfare Queens, and Cheaters

The crack epidemic caught the attention of health officials, law enforcement, social service agencies, education professionals, and addiction researchers. One particular reason was the disproportionately large numbers of female users. Historically, most illegal drug abusers have been male.[18]

This pattern was broken during the 1980s when, for the first time, large numbers of women began using illicit drugs.[19] Women were more inclined to use crack cocaine because it was inexpensive, painless to use (smoked rather than injected), and easily accessible. These women generally were between the ages of eighteen and twenty-five, most had no prior drug abuse record, and many bore children with a positive cocaine toxicology.

Public reaction to crack-abusing women was embedded in the political and cultural climate of the decade. Conservatives argued that the Great Society social programs of the 1960s were not the solutions to poverty, but had become part of the problem. They argued that these policies destroyed families, diffused immorality, increased taxes, maintained welfare rolls, and lowered productivity among the poor.[20] Such claims resulted in disillusionment with the social welfare system, and conservative ideas about Aid to Families with Dependent Children (AFDC) gained popularity. Ultimately, Republicans aimed to freeze government spending on those who were considered undeserving because of their individual moral choices and who thus had become a burden to taxpayers. President Reagan frequently referred to single women receiving public assistance as "welfare queens" and "cheaters"—AFDC recipients who robbed the system.[21]

Equally influential was Charles Murray's 1984 publication of *Losing Ground,* a book aimed at challenging the effectiveness of social policies that targeted poor women with dependent children.[22] Murray set out to provide empirical evidence of the failure of such programs; arguing that illegitimacy was at the root of all social problems, he assailed AFDC and similar programs for their promotion of immoral lifestyles.[23] When discussing the impact of *Losing Ground* on the Reagan administration, Katz explained:

> Murray's argument fit the Reagan agenda perfectly. At precisely the appropriate moment, it provided what appeared to be an authoritative rationale for reducing social benefits and dismantling affirmative action. Nearly every reviewer commented on Murray's influence. In March 1985, Robert Greenstein observed "Congress will soon engage in bitter battles over where to cut the federal budget, and *Losing Ground* is already being used as ammunition by those who would direct more reductions at programs for the poor." Murray's name, pointed out Christopher Jencks, "has been invoked repeatedly in Washington's current debate over the budget—not because he has provided new evidence on the effects of particular government programs, but because he is widely presumed to have proven that federal social policy as a whole made the poor worse off over the past twenty years." *Losing Ground,* others pointed out was the Reagan administration's new Bible.[24]

Murray's work helped justify federal reductions in programs for AFDC families—the so-called undeserving poor. Eighty-five percent of the cutbacks were made in food stamp and nutrition programs, and another 40 percent were made in Medicare.[25]

This attitude toward the poor ultimately affected public perceptions of crack-abusing women. Crack mothers were considered part of the undeserving poor and a new social problem. As was the case with other AFDC recipients, these women's children had become another responsibility for the American taxpayer. Like the sociopolitically created "welfare queen," crack mothers were portrayed as being sexually irresponsible, neglecting their children, and using government funds to support their addiction.[26] Newspaper articles reinforced the burden of caring for crack-exposed babies, with headlines such as "U.S. Health Care Crisis in the Making: Staggering Number of Drug Addicted Infants Strain Facilities";[27] "Crack Spreads Fear and Frustration, Overwhelming Hospitals"; and "Their Mothers Used Drugs, and Now It's the Children Who Suffer."[28] Americans began to resent the responsibility for crack babies—the offspring of poor inner-city drug-abusing women. Hostility toward crack mothers ultimately won wide public support for the antidrug crusade. This support was demonstrated by public opinion polls, which indicated that more than 60 percent of Americans surveyed believed that drugs were the biggest challenge facing the nation, even if it was not a major issue in their hometowns.[29]

Punitive Policies, Social Welfare, and Gender-Specific Drug Treatment

Outrage about prenatal drug exposure stigmatized crack-abusing women. However, their drug-exposed infants continued to win the sympathy of the public. As a result, drug-impacted families became the focus of social policy during the late 1980s and early 1990s. Focusing on the shortcomings of drug-abusing parents, such initiatives aimed to address prenatal substance abuse in the context of child welfare policy. As expected, these policies were governed by initiatives directed toward the "war on drugs" and the "undeserving poor." The stereotypes of crack-abusing mothers as women who had lost their maternal instincts were equally influential.

Frustrations with crack mothers resulted in punitive policies that affected mainly lower-class Black and Latina women. Public health officials enforced mandatory reporting requirements, allowing the testing of women who were suspected of using drugs while pregnant, and crack-exposed babies were taken away from their mothers after birth. However, this practice was implemented only in public hospitals. Race and class privileges protected middle-class White women using private hospitals, and their prenatal drug abuse was much more easily overlooked. Research has shown that women using public hospitals were ten times more likely to be reported to authorities.[30] By the end of the decade, punitive initiatives escalated to the level of criminal prosecutions.[31] More than two hundred women in thirty different states were criminally charged for exposing their babies to drugs during pregnancy.[32]

The criminalization of prenatal substance abuse started a national dialogue between policy makers and legal scholars, social workers, women's rights advocates, and child protective agencies. The key issues were: Are drug-abusing women liable for the damage done to their fetus or newborn? Should babies be taken away from their mothers on the basis of a positive drug test alone? What are the rights of the mother with regard to privacy? Does the state have a role in protecting an unborn child? And if the state should intervene, what should be the extent and nature of its involvement?

Organizations such as the National Association of Social Workers, the American Medical Association, the American Bar Association, and the American Society of Addiction Medicine opposed punitive sanctions and advocated for better drug treatment interventions. They pointed out that criminalizing the disease would not stop pregnant women from using drugs. Punishing crack mothers is predicated on the belief that people with addictions can stop their problematic behavior instantly. Prosecutors, they argued, were ignoring other important psychosocial dimensions of the disease.

Drug treatment ultimately became the number one priority on the social policy agenda. But many existing programs refused to admit pregnant women. Furthermore, programs that were accessible used paradigms designed for male participants, overlooking the specific needs of women in general and pregnant women in particular. The American Civil Liberties Union (ACLU) testified on behalf of women in a hearing on the effectiveness of drug treatment programs.[33] They discussed how things such as prenatal care and child care services were missing in treatment services for women, and how these things are essential for successful outcomes.[34]

For example, researchers at the Columbia University School of Public Health surveyed the quality of services provided to women in programs in New York City. They found that 95 percent of the programs (approximately seventy-eight programs) had no services specifically for women; 54 percent refused to treat women who were expecting; 67 percent denied treatment services to pregnant women on Medicaid; 87 percent had no available services for pregnant women addicted to crack who were Medicaid-eligible; and 44 percent did not provide prenatal care for pregnant women.[35]

Courts began mandating family service plans, which required drug-abusing mothers to successfully complete substance abuse treatment. However, the social stigma attached to crack mothers and the fear of criminal prosecutions deterred many substance-abusing women from seeking drug treatment and appropriate prenatal health care, even when services were available. Consequently, more younger children were placed into the foster care system during the 1990s, causing foster home shortages in major U.S. cities such as Newark, New York, Chicago, and Washington, D.C.[36] The United States Department of Health and Human Services reported that since the 1980s 23 percent of all children entering foster care were under the age of one year, an increase from 12 percent in 1977.[37] Most of these cases involved substantiated reports of child abuse and neglect by a substance-abusing parent.[38]

This rise in foster care placement was also attributed to other factors. Although prenatal drug exposure includes a variety of substances, social service agencies classified crack-involved families as extremely high-risk. These cases were treated more seriously for two specific reasons: First, crack cocaine was highly addictive and was used predominantly in poor urban neighborhoods. Therefore, social workers believed that supporting the habit drained more household resources, making children more vulnerable to neglect and malnourishment.[39] Second, the drug was associated with a dramatic rise in criminal activity, which placed children in greater danger. As a result, many children in drug-affected families were immediately removed from their homes.[40]

Responding to the breakdown of families affected by substance abuse, Congress approved the funds for the establishment of family preservation programs in 1993. These programs were developed under the theory that intensive, short-term interventions would better serve families in crisis, eventually reducing the number of out-of-home placements. However, the combination of addiction and poverty left social workers at their wits' end; these families were new to the system, and agencies had little information to help them tackle the myriad issues resulting from crack abuse.[41] Many veteran social workers began leaving their jobs, and less experienced replacements were expected to pick up the slack, which resulted in mismanaged cases.[42] In addition, such preservation designs were originally developed for families with mental health issues and were largely ineffective with cases involving drug-abusing parents.[43] Essentially, the social service system was unsuccessful in meeting the needs of substance-abuse-affected families during the crack era.

The Post-Crack Era: Current Public Policies and Attitudes Affecting Poor Drug-Impacted Families

Toward the end of the 1990s, most of the policies aimed at convicting women for exposing their babies to drugs were voted down. Organized campaigns against the national trend of prosecuting crack mothers were successful. Women were charged, but very few actually did jail time. Some states continued to push for criminal sanctions, which brought attention back to issues regarding race, class, and substance abuse during pregnancy. In a 2001 high-profile case, the Center for Reproductive Law and Policy (CRLP) challenged the constitutionality of drug tests for women in public hospitals. *Ferguson v. City of Charleston* actually began in 1993, when nine women were arrested and two jailed for testing positive for drugs after delivery at the University of South Carolina Medical Center.[44] The medical center adopted its reporting policy in 1989, allowing drug testing of pregnant women without their consent. The CRLP argued that not only was this practice unconstitutional, but poor minority women were the major victims. After a civil rights investigation led by the Department of Health and Human Services demonstrated that most of the women charged were African American, the hospital agreed to discontinue the practice.

However, the legality of drug testing resulted in a series of court battles. The University of South Carolina Medical Center's policy was upheld in federal court in 1996, and again in 1999 by the U.S. Court of Appeals, Fourth Circuit. The CRLP subsequently filed a petition with the Supreme Court, and oral arguments began in October 2000.[45] Attorneys for the medical center argued that the state has an obligation to protect unborn babies from drug exposure. Attorneys for the CRLP built their case on the premise that such a policy violates the Fourth Amendment right to protection from unreasonable searches. Reactions to defending women who expose their fetuses to drugs were mixed. However, in February 2001, in a 6–3 decision, the Supreme Court ruled that testing without consent (and subsequent prosecution) is unconstitutional.

The trajectory of punitive policies continues, however. Such penalties are inherent in welfare laws, social service practices, and other legislative policies. These reforms were implemented to deny benefits to families with a history of drug involvement in general, and drug abuse during pregnancy in particular. For instance, lawmakers implemented civil child abuse legislation mandating the termination of parental rights if children are exposed to controlled substances, if babies are adversely affected as a result of drug exposure, or if children are not receiving proper care as a result of their parent's substance abuse.[46] These laws were written under the pretext of being in the best interest of the children. However, they are equivalent to criminal sanctions in that they are punitive and will inadvertently discourage mothers from seeking help for their addiction.

Public Law 104-193, the Personal Responsibility and Work Opportunity Reconciliation Act, enacted on August 22, 1996, also included penalties for drug-impacted families that will ultimately affect dependent children. This reform replaced the traditional AFDC program with a system of accountability offering only Temporary Assistance for Needy Families (TANF).

Section 115 of the bill threatens the livelihood of dependent families by punishing parents with a history of drug involvement.[47] This provision made individuals with drug-related convictions ineligible for assistance under TANF and food stamp programs. Women could lose benefits if they or any other household member is convicted for a drug-related offense.

Although this law was written to target only those convicted for drug-related offenses, it further demonstrates the biases against poor families impacted by parental drug abuse. For instance, from 1986 to 1996 the number of females arrested for drug-related offenses increased by 95 percent.[48] By 1998 an estimated 272,073 more women had been arrested for drug-related crimes,[49] mostly nonviolent offenses.[50] Although murderers, child molesters, and other offenders commit more serious crimes, these categories are not mentioned in this provision to deny public assistance.

Statistics on the prevalence of drug abuse in AFDC families also demonstrates the impact of these policies. Ninety-five percent of adults receiving benefits are female heads of household, and women on AFDC are more likely to abuse substances in comparison to those not receiving benefits.[51] Such penalties will also affect the possibility of drug treatment, inasmuch as AFDC benefits usually cover the cost.[52] Furthermore, AFDC women with substance abuse problems are less likely to find stable employment in comparison to women without substance abuse issues.[53]

The first national report examining the impact of the lifetime welfare ban on drug-abusing women was recently published. The report shows that since 1996, ninety-two thousand women have been denied welfare benefits under this law.[54] The report was only able to gather data from twenty-three states. However, it notes that forty-two are fully or partially enforcing the ban.[55] Twenty-two states deny benefits entirely, ten deny them partially, and in ten others benefits are based on participation in a drug-treatment program.[56] Seven other states and the District of Columbia have chosen not to participate.[57] Consistent with the statistics on women convicted for drug-related offenses, the report also pointed out that African-American and Latina women are disproportionately affected. For instance, African-American women are overrepresented in the states of Alabama, Delaware, Illinois, Mississippi, Pennsylvania, and Virginia.[58] States with an overrepresentation of Latina women include Arizona and California.[59] This report also demonstrates that children are the most vulnerable victims of the welfare ban. It points out that 135,000 children are at risk because without the support of public assistance, their parents will be unable to properly care for them.

The failures of the social service system during the crack era left many children lingering in foster care. At the end of the 1990s, 550,000 children were in the system, a dramatic increase since the mid-1980s.[60] As a remedy, Congress passed Public Law 105-89, the Adoption and Safe Families Act, in November 1997. Originally Public Law 96-272, the Adoption Assistance and Child Welfare Act of 1980, this law was designed to find permanent placement for foster children who remained in the system after a twelve-to-fifteen-month period. Advocates argued that too much emphasis was placed on addressing the needs of the biological parent, which resulted in a foster care crisis. The law was written to replace the popular family preservation intervention that was ineffective with drug-impacted families during the late 1980s and early 1990s. Enacted on the philosophy that adoption, as opposed to long-term foster care, is in the best interest of the child, families are offered financial assistance to adopt children.

The Adoption and Safe Families Act has made it easier to place children from drug-affected families for adoption—in contrast to family preservation policies, reasonable efforts to preserve the family are not required under the Adoption and Safe Families Act. As a result, parents needing more intensive drug treatment are less likely to place their children in temporary care, for fear of losing custody permanently. In addition, if sobriety is not achieved in the specified amount of time, mothers who could benefit from more-intensive treatment services could still lose custody of their children.

The Adoption and Safe Families Act has resulted in other unintended consequences. The challenges of rearing drug-affected youngsters have made it difficult for states to secure permanent placements. Foster parents reported that many of these children were unusually hyperactive, had pre-existing medical conditions, and suffered from severe emotional trauma. These things overwhelmed many families, making it difficult to find consistent caretakers for this population.[61] Other variables have also contributed to the difficulty in securing adoptive homes. Most children needing placement are older, are of color, and are part of a sibling group, which makes finding permanent homes more difficult.[62] These groups are much harder to place. As a result, although parental rights have been terminated in the best interest of the children, many have not been adopted and will grow up in the foster care system. At the end of the 1990s, forty-four thousand children were still waiting for permanent placements.

Since advocates for pregnant drug-abusing women have demonstrated the need for more specialized treatment modalities, substance abuse programs have expanded their services to respond to the particular needs of women, including mothers with children. However, funding for gender-specific models is far below the demand for services.[63] The Substance Abuse and Mental Health Services Administration (SAMHSA) allocated funding for demonstration programs during the early 1990s. However, toward the end of the decade funding for these programs decreased substantially.[64]

Substance abuse services in the United States have also been crippled by the trend toward managed health care.[65] Under this system, the responsibility for making decisions regarding treatment services shifted from clinicians to insurance companies. With the goal of cutting the cost of services, these companies have focused on short-term services. However, research has shown that long-term residential treatment modalities will produce better outcomes.[66] The majority of drug-abusing pregnant women are polysubstance users, who require more-intensive in-patient regimens.[67] A report to the American Society of Addiction Medicine explained the pitfalls of leaving addiction treatment decisions to non-health-care-professionals:

> While the healthcare community might be more inclined to see motivational difficulties as a part of the very symptom of addictive disorder, the insurance industry is more likely to take the position that a negative attitude represents a "lifestyle choice," thereby forfeiting the prospective patient's right to health insurance benefits.[68]

Therefore, even though substance abuse services have made improvements, many women with children do not receive the appropriate treatment due to conflicts with insurance providers. These issues remain major obstacles for drug treatment programs that are focused on serving pregnant women and mothers with children.

More-intensive treatment will also cut the medical costs associated with drug-impacted babies. For instance, a Florida study showed that drug-exposed newborns have a higher incidence of major medical needs.[69] In 1997, 77 percent of drug-exposed babies had costly medical needs, in comparison to 27 percent of all newborns. The average cost for one drug-exposed infant was over $11,000. This leaves the total cost of drug-exposed infants in Florida estimated at $6.7 million. A study by the Johns Hopkins University School of Medicine demonstrates that providing treatment to drug-abusing women who are pregnant significantly reduced the health care needs of their infants.[70] Therefore, it is less costly for the managed health care system to provide adequate care to drug-abusing women while pregnant than to treat their infants after they have been exposed. Insufficient treatment modalities will only continue to drive up medical costs and will not produce the desired outcomes for families impacted by drug abuse.

Sterilizing Drug-Abusing Parents: A Growing National Campaign

"Don't Let a Pregnancy Ruin Your Drug Habit."
"If You Use Drugs, Get Birth Control, Get $200 Cash."[71]

Public interest in crack-abusing women and drug-exposed babies began to fade away during the mid-1990s. The sins of "crack mothers" and "welfare queens" were no longer the focus of news stories. Drug-exposed infants had also disappeared from the mainstream media—their developmental problems were no longer major media concern. Simultaneously, images of the popular urban crack subculture also began to vanish. Although drug addiction continued to devastate inner-city communities, strong law enforcement tactics had dismantled many drug-peddling street organizations, and the American public lost interest in the popular "war on drugs" narratives. However, at the end of the 1990s parental drug addiction continued to present challenges to child welfare services. As the same time, public concern regarding the responsibility for drug-affected children resurged, drawing attention back to the morality of using drugs while pregnant and the societal burden posed by children of substance-abusing parents.

As discussed, several new punitive policy interventions were created during the late 1990s. Such initiatives were directed toward families with substance abuse problems who were dependent on the welfare system. Criminalizing prenatal substance abuse was no longer an acceptable option. However, those who believe that prenatal substance abuse represented a character flaw continued to push for stronger intervention tactics. As a result, efforts to prosecute crack-abusing women have now been replaced by an even more controversial sterilization campaign. This alternative intervention method is at the center of the discussions regarding parental drug addiction in general, and prenatal substance abuse in particular.

Similar to the criminalization of prenatal substance abuse, the controversy surrounding the movement to sterilize drug abusing women has been discussed on television news shows, in popular magazines, and on radio talk shows in most major cities. The publicity given to this topic has emphasized the benefits of using birth control while struggling with drug addiction. However, there are many concerns regarding the ethics of a program designed to sterilize poor women with substance abuse problems, and these are rarely examined in detail.

The idea to begin sterilizing drug-abusing women became popular toward the end of the 1990s. The movement was started in 1997 by Barbara Harris, a foster mother who adopted a sibling group of eight children whose mother used drugs. Four of the eight children were born prenatally exposed to crack. During the early 1990s Harris had also lobbied to pass legislation that would make pregnant drug-abusing women accountable for the adverse outcomes of their babies. When these efforts were unsuccessful, she started Project Prevention, also known as C.R.A.C.K. (Children Requiring a Caring Kommunity), an organization with the mission of preventing drug-abusing parents from having children, thus relieving the American taxpayer of the responsibility of caring for these children.

While addiction treatment specialists and medical professionals have criticized the idea of sterilizing parents with substance abuse problems, the project leaders have stressed the fact that their clients are not forced into the program. The decision to participate in the program is left to the discretion of the drug-abusing parents themselves. However, C.R.A.C.K. recruiting activities are focused primarily on substance abuse treatment programs and health clinics serving pregnant drug-abusing women. Project Prevention offers drug-abusing men and women a monetary incentive not to reproduce. Participants are paid a $200 payment to provide evidence of long-term birth control or sterilization. Although temporary birth control is offered as an option, the project encourages sterilization for drug-abusing parents. Tubal ligation is suggested for the women, and men are encouraged to volunteer for a vasectomy.

C.R.A.C.K. has already reached cities that have the highest incidences of drug-exposed births, such as Chicago, Baltimore, Washington, D.C., Los Angeles, Houston, Seattle, Las Vegas, Dallas, St. Louis, Denver, Pittsburgh, Atlanta, San Diego, and Cleveland.[72]

The acceptance of a campaign to sterilize drug-abusing women is another example of the societal stigma attached to poor women with substance abuse problems. Although the campaign also offers birth control to drug-abusing men, it is mainly directed toward pregnant women and mothers with children. The organization's leaders defend the existence of the program by noting that the number of pregnant women and mothers with children who are drug abusers continues to grow. The shortage of foster and adoptive homes for these children and the rising cost of special education in drug-impacted school districts are also a major highlight of the campaign. This information is used to remind the public that the problem of drug-abusing women with dependent children is an ongoing one and to highlight the burden of caring for drug-affected children.

The organization has also pointed out that women who use crack are not the focus of the campaign. However, although many pregnant drug-abusing women have been found to use a combination of substances, including alcohol, the organization has adopted the acronym C.R.A.C.K., which is associated with the urban drug epidemic and crack-exposed babies. Using the name C.R.A.C.K. has helped the project gain popularity among many conservatives and has also helped it win the support of major financial donors. It is unlikely that a program focusing on sterilizing substance-abusing parents would use the acronym A.L.C.O.H.O.L., even though alcohol causes more neurological damage to children than crack cocaine. In addition, children in families affected by alcohol are just as likely to be physically abused, and emotionally neglected.[73] Substances such as tobacco, marijuana, or other drugs are even less likely to be highlighted as part of a sterilization campaign.

The vulnerability of drug abusers with limited resources speaks to the ethics of using cash incentives to encourage sterilization of drug abusers. Pregnant substance abusers in more economically stable families have better financial resources to support their habit. Therefore, they are less likely to be motivated to give up their reproductive freedoms for a $200 cash incentive. Poor drug-impacted families struggle to provide adequate food, clothing, and shelter while supporting the addicted member's habit. It is unlikely that such an important reproductive decision can be made thoughtfully under such circumstances.

Some members of the medical community and other advocates for drug-abusing women question the legitimacy of the notion of *voluntary participation* in the context of economically vulnerable women with substance abuse problems. Voluntary participation requires patients to give their informed consent—meaning that participation is uncoerced and that the patient is fully aware of the pros and cons of the program.[74] Sterilization programs that are Medicaid-sponsored requires that a consent form be signed by the participant, demonstrating that he or she has been given adequate medical information regarding the procedure.[75] Considering the nature of addictive behavior and the financial need of this population, it is difficult to determine whether informed consent is being obtained under the C.R.A.C.K. program.

The Committee on Women, Population, and the Environment (CWPE) and National Advocates for Pregnant Women have highlighted other noteworthy facts about C.R.A.C.K. Most importantly, they pointed out that the program supports negative stereotypes of crack-exposed babies. Its messages suggest that poor drug-abusing women are producing a biologically inferior group of people and that population control methods are needed to address this problem. However, current and more sophisticatedly designed studies of drug-exposed babies and developmental outcomes challenged this assumption. Studies have found that although prenatal drug exposure does result in result in some adverse outcomes, most of these children are not permanently damaged and with appropriately designed early interventions could develop normally.[76] Furthermore, as the chapter on drug-exposed children and special education policy explains, this population has not necessarily been made eligible for special education services. Therefore, although some of these children have developmental issues that need to be addressed, they are not solely responsible for the escalating cost of special education.

Organizations against sterilizing drug-abusing women have also analyzed this campaign in the context of the eugenics movement. Sterilization laws enacted during the 1930s were predicted on the belief that "undesirable" populations should not be allowed to procreate.[77] Under this philosophy, sterilization laws were enacted in twenty-seven states, affecting

Native Americans, African Americans, the mentally and physically challenged, and the poor.[78] An estimated 100,000 to 150,000 low-income women were sterilized by 1970.[79] These women were coerced to participate by the threat that their public aid would be discontinued.[80] By 1974, the United States District Court in Washington, D.C., ruled that such practices were unethical and were to be abolished.[81]

Most importantly, CWPE and other addiction treatment professionals pointed out that C.R.A.C.K.'s goals are in direct contrast to the goals of substance abuse treatment. The project does not offer drug treatment options, fails to encourage healthy sexual practices, and does not promote use of highly effective, less controversial methods of birth control such as condoms, which also protect against HIV and other sexually transmitted diseases common among drug-abusing populations. Drug-abusing women who also live in poverty are at high risk for sexual health problems. They are also less likely to seek and receive appropriate medical care during their addiction. Birth control methods such as Norplant and Depo-Provera, which are offered as medium-term solutions, have side effects that could aggravate the health problems associated with drug addiction.[82] These birth control devices will also put more chemicals in the bodies of women, whose systems are already ravaged by drugs.

Summary and Conclusions

Prenatal substance abuse gained national attention during the crack era. However, the attention had less to do with concern for drug-exposed babies than with the sentiments directed toward poor drug-abusing women and the burden their children could present to society. Although providing more gender-specific drug treatment programs and better prenatal care for drug-abusing women was discusssed, these issues were not major concerns. Even less attention was given to actually meeting the growth and developmental needs of drug-affected infants after they are born.[83] The bulk of federal monies were allocated to interdiction, eradication, and law enforcement efforts.[84] This is surprising inasmuch as research supports the conclusion that law enforcement efforts are more costly than developing effective treatment services.[85]

More much attention has been given to the treatment needs of pregnant drug-abusing women in the past decade. However, societal attitudes toward crack-abusing women have not changed—these women continue to be stigmatized, and most social policy interventions remain punitive in nature. "Crack mothers" from low-income communities are no different from middle-class women who struggle with substance abuse issues—they are equally concerned about the potential harm to their babies. However, the combination of addiction and poverty creates symptoms that are more difficult for poorer families to overcome.

To adequately address addiction among pregnant women or mothers with children from socioeconomically challenged communities, societal attitudes toward this population must change. If not, we will continue to invest in solutions that will only create bigger problems in the long term. More emphasis must be placed on building better support systems for drug-impacted families and addressing the specific developmental needs of children who are affected. This includes focusing more on specialized drug treatment services for women with school-age children, targeting drug-abusing pregnant women for special prenatal care programs, and designing special early intervention educational programs for drug-affected children and their parents.

The C.R.A.C.K. organization would do a better job of reducing the societal burden posed by children of drug-abusing parents by adopting practices that will strengthen these families. Such interventions could assist parents in gaining the skills and opportunities necessary to be responsible for their own children, which includes offering job training, educational opportunities, access to effective early intervention, mental health services, and affordable and decent housing and child care services. These things will ultimately improve the quality of life for the children, eliminating the need for foster care placement, extensive medical care, and special education.

The best interest of the children is served by addressing prenatal drug exposure and parental drug addiction in a public health context. Efforts currently devoted to a sterilization campaign and punitive interventions should be directed instead toward promoting healthy sexual practices among drug-abusing women and encouraging their participation in addiction treatment services, ultimately contributing to the healthy growth and development of their children.

CHAPTER 2

Drug-Exposed Children and Development

What Has the Research Taught Us?

Introduction

Drug-exposed children came of school age in the late 1980s and early 1990s. After all the media hype about drug-exposed infants and developmental adversities, no one was exactly sure what to expect from these children. Educators had many questions: What were schools to do with crack babies? Would these children be mentally retarded? Would they act like uncontrollable monsters? What were their intellectual capabilities? How would schools teach this population? How much special education funding would be allocated for them? Are existing special education programs designed to address their needs? Would crack exposed children need an alternative educational setting? The school-age crack kid was a new educational phenomenon. Most importantly, researchers were predicting that in some inner-city school districts, 40 to 60 percent of the children were prenatally exposed to drugs.[1]

Accordingly, news stories turned away from a focus on the strain on the health care and social service systems and began to concentrate on the problems these children would present to public schools. Stories about school-age drug-exposed children began to appear in the educational literature. Warnings appeared in journal articles with titles such as "Crack Babies: Here They Come, Ready or Not," "'Crack Babies' in the Classroom," "Crack Babies Turn 5 and Schools Brace," and "Crack Babies' in School".[2] One article stated that "perhaps most frightening of all is that doctors and other health professionals can only speculate about what we may be facing."[3] Another suggested that "urban schools would be pressed to the limit trying to teach the flood of children born to mothers who used crack."[4]

Medical research studies were beginning to confirm some of these suspicions; the developmental prognosis for drug-exposed children was grim. Studies of crack-exposed children were reporting that the drug caused a myriad of developmental abnormalities in infants, citing poor brain growth, failure to thrive, deficiencies in motor development, overstimulation, delayed language development, and atypical social interactions. These things, researchers predicted, would result in severe learning disabilities later in life, which had implications for public school systems. Other reports argued that crack had produced a generation of children doomed for life—a biological underclass. Despite these assumptions, there had been little progress in determining the long-term effects of crack exposure. Although studies had demonstrated that drug exposure resulted in some impairment, knowledge about the needs of school-age children was lacking. Would these crack-exposed youngsters outgrow their developmental challenges, or would these problems get worse?

Since the mid-1980s, the effect of crack exposure on development has been one of the most debated topics in the study of prenatal drug abuse. While research had been done on exposure to other drugs in utero, crack cocaine was a new substance; it was smoked rather than injected, and many believed that this could probably do more damage to the developing fetus. Public concern for crack-exposed babies spurred researchers to learn more about how this condition actually affected children. However, studying crack-exposed babies was more challenging for investigators—designing studies that would adequately answer questions about the effects of the exposure was almost impossible. Most crack-abusing mothers lived in an unhealthy subculture, which made it extremely difficult for researchers to determine if the drug alone was the major cause of abnormalities in their children. No longitudinal research had been conducted, and information on school-age children was virtually nonexistent. Furthermore, clinical studies had started to produce contradictory conclusions, some arguing that "crack baby syndrome" was a scientific myth that had become a self-fulfilling prophecy.[5]

A recently published meta-analysis examined the large body of literature regarding prenatal cocaine exposure and problems in development. Published in the March 2001 edition of the *Journal of the American Medical Association (JAMA)*, the study analyzed articles that appeared from 1984 to 2000. Only thirty-six of seventy-four of the studies obtained met the inclusion requirements.[6] The other thirty-eight were excluded on the basis of serious methodological flaws. The investigators concluded that,

based on this analysis of previous studies, there was "no consistent negative association between prenatal cocaine exposure and physical growth,
developmental test scores, or receptive or expressive language."[7] They also
noted that "no independent cocaine effects have been shown on standardized parent and teacher reports of child behaviors scored by an accepted
criteria," concluding that there is still no scientific evidence that links
crack cocaine directly to adverse outcomes.[8] This study reopened public
discussions regarding the impact of drug exposure on the development of
children.

Reviewing the medical research regarding crack-exposed children and
developmental outcomes is important to this overall discussion. Although
there is an abundance of literature about the effects of prenatal drug exposure, for various reasons (most of which will be discussed in this chapter) it
has been more difficult for medical researchers to draw any definite conclusions about crack exposure and developmental outcomes. This population has been the most complex to understand in the context of how the
drug impedes overall intellectual functioning. However, before any serious
consideration can be given to the policy and intervention needs of schoolchildren, this literature must be examined and discussed in a manner that
explains the different research trajectories. It is also important to conduct
the review in the context of what scientific studies have confirmed and
ruled out about the adverse effects of prenatal crack exposure. As subsequent chapters will point out, this research is directly related to how policy
makers and schools have responded to these children.

This chapter begins with a review of literature on the developmental
outcomes of drug-exposed children. As you will see, there are many misunderstandings about children born prenatally exposed to drugs, particularly those who are referred to as "crack babies." In addition to explaining
the challenges of studying the effects of prenatal drug exposure, also discussed are efforts to improve research in this area. The influence of other
risk factors such as quality of prenatal care, maternal health, use of multiple substances, and other environmental circumstances are also discussed.

The Debate about Crack Baby Syndrome

The adverse effects of prenatal crack exposure were first reported in the
medical literature in 1983.[9] However, the first widely cited study was led by
Dr. Ira Chasnoff and published in the *New England Journal of Medicine* in
1985.[10] Comparing drug-exposed and nonexposed infants, Dr. Chasnoff
and associates noticed more abnormalities in the exposed group, suggesting that crack exposure might be more harmful to infants than previously
thought. According to the researchers, crack-exposed babies demonstrated

significant depression on interactive behavior and poor organizational response to environmental stimuli.[11] This 1985 study was the first linking prenatal crack exposure to abnormal outcomes; it sparked new interest among medical researchers regarding substance abuse during pregnancy, particularly abuse of the popular new street drug crack. Until then, most studies on prenatal substance abuse had focused on tobacco, marijuana, heroin, and alcohol exposure. However, low public expectations for crack babies attracted unprecedented attention to prenatal substance abuse, particularly among poor urban women.

Following the 1985 study, a series of articles reported prematurity, small gestational age, poor motor performance, low cognitive abilities, behavioral problems, physical abnormalities, and other major health problems.[12] As these reports burgeoned, crack baby syndrome became a widely discussed topic in medical and pediatric journals. Appearing at the height of the media reporting of the urban drug baby epidemic, such reports supported public resentment toward poor drug-abusing mothers. While the studies only reported developmental abnormalities and did not demonstrate permanent disabilities in these children, to some they validated the belief that poor urban drug-abusing women were producing a new, biologically inferior segment of society.

Unexpectedly, research on drug-exposed babies changed focus during the 1990s. Some investigators challenged the early results, suggesting that crack baby syndrome was a result of media hype and political rhetoric. They suggested that the stereotypical images of crack-abusing mothers and their babies were influencing how researchers reported the adversities found in drug-exposed infants. City newspapers begin reporting on the new findings regarding the overdramatization of crack babies, with headlines such as "The Myth of the Crack Babies" and "Crack Babies: The Worst Threat Is Mom Herself."[13]

One widely cited article published in the *Journal of the American Medical Association*, was entitled "The Problem with Prenatal Cocaine Exposure: A Rush to Judgment" and fueled the debate regarding the research on babies exposed to crack and other drugs.[14] The article acknowledged that studies on the effects of crack exposure were full of serious methodological problems and suggested that existing assumptions about these children be reexamined. Leading researchers, including Chasnoff himself, took a second look at the findings of previous studies and agreed that the fears about crack-exposed babies might have been exaggerated. Other factors, they believed, could be equally responsible for the developmental impairments found in infants who had been exposed to drugs, particularly crack cocaine. According to critics, although impairments were detected, the studies did not demonstrate a direct association between crack and the abnormalities. Most importantly, the expected severe neurological damage was not present. These concerns were just as captivating as the initial stories of crack baby syndrome, and the public became equally involved in this debate.

The reliability of earlier studies was challenged on two important grounds. First, crack-abusing women are overwhelmingly poor and less likely to have had adequate prenatal care. They have high incidences of sexually transmitted diseases, including hepatitis B, gonorrhea, and AIDS; usually they have poor diets, and they are more likely to live in chaotic, unstable environments.[15] These circumstances will ultimately affect the development of children regardless of prenatal drug exposure. Therefore, researchers argued, these factors may be primarily responsible for the adversities found in crack-exposed children, particularly those who remain in the care of their biological parents. Second is the issue of polydrug use among pregnant crack-abusing women. Although crack usually is the drug of choice, many use a combination of other substances, including alcohol, marijuana, and tobacco, which could also be contributing to developmental impairments. A 1989 study published by the National Association for Perinatal Addiction Research and Education supported this finding. The study surveyed thirty-six hospitals nationwide and found that about 11 percent of women who delivered in those hospitals had used a variety of drugs. Furthermore, most studies on the impact of drug exposure on developmental outcomes had failed to include an appropriate control group. For these reasons, the medical community has concluded that it is irresponsible to identify crack exposure alone as the major cause of abnormalities in children.[16]

Drug-exposed youngsters were continuing to demonstrate developmental difficulties. However, concerns regarding study design and methodological rigor were taking research in a new direction. Investigators began to study these children in the context of the aforementioned risk factors, in addition to exposure to crack cocaine and other substances. These new investigations provided a more rounded picture of the developmental issues affecting drug-exposed children. Newly conducted studies had shown that although drug exposure places these children at risk, most still demonstrated normal intellectual capabilities, concluding that postnatal circumstances are a better predictor of developmental outcomes.[17] The reports provided solid evidence that although prenatal exposure to crack could lead to delays, these children are not necessarily doomed for life—the impairments could be corrected.

For instance, a three-year longitudinal study on the developmental outcomes of drug-exposed children compared three different groups of children: polydrug-exposed, including cocaine; polydrug-exposed, but no cocaine; and nonexposed.[18] Both groups of children in the exposed categories scored significantly lower than the non-exposed comparison group and the cocaine exposure was found to be a predictor of poor verbal reasoning, demonstrating that children who are prenatally exposed to drugs are vulnerable to developmental challenges later in life.[19] However, the results showed subtle differences in overall scores between the exposed and nonexposed children on the Stanford-Binet Intelligence Scale. Similarly, Hurt and colleagues observed 101 cocaine-exposed newborns through the first thirty months of life. Their developmental outcomes were compared to a control group of 118 nonexposed babies. At the end of thirty months, the drug-exposed children had lower weights and smaller head sizes. However, there was no significant difference between the groups in mental development index and psychomotor development index scores on the Bayley Scales of Infant Development, challenging the belief that crack exposure resulted in permanent developmental adversities.[20]

These new findings became the reference for discussions about crack-exposed children and developmental outcomes. They helped downplay the stereotypes about crack babies as a group of children with drug-related physical and mental deformities and offered educators a reason for optimism in working with these youngsters. Such findings had unintended consequences, however, in that they began to turn attention away from the developmental needs of children born prenatally exposed to drugs. Although this continued to be a problem from a public health and social service perspective, educational professionals were beginning to pay less attention to this issue. This worked against the best interest of children inasmuch as schools did not focus specifically on the academic needs of students affected by drug exposure.

These studies predicted that drug-exposed babies could reach developmentally appropriate levels of achievement. However, many of these children were still lagging behind their peers developmentally. Their intelligence test scores were within the normal range, but most were at the low end of the scale, demonstrating that they were an extremely fragile group of children that needed special attention. For instance, one study pointed out that there were no overall mean differences between drug-exposed children and their socioeconomically equivalent peers on the commonly used Bayley Scales of Infant Development. However, the exposed group had a higher percentage of IQ scores that were at least two standard deviations below the mean.[21]

Essentially, just as research could not prove that crack alone was responsible for the adversities detected in children and that these youngsters were capable of normal intellectual functioning, drug exposure could not be totally ruled out as a contributing factor in their developmental difficulties. As a result, although research in this area had made noteworthy strides, the question of how or if crack itself affects outcomes remained a clinical research concern. Are drug-exposed children really any different from their peers with developmental challanges? If so, how? If not, what is the root of their problems? Are risk factors such as prenatal care, the use of multiple substances, and the lifestyles of their drug-abusing parents the major cause? Why are these children continuing to demonstrate developmental delays?

Controlling for Other Variables: Environmental Risk Factors, Maternal Health, and Polydrug Use

Such contrasting results left classroom teachers and educational policy makers befuddled; they were still uncertain about what to expect from the drug-affected population.[22] If educational policies and programs were to be designed in the best interest of drug-exposed schoolchildren, education professionals needed to know how these children differed from other youngsters from challenged environments. Research on the topic was unclear and contradictory. Crack did not kill these children's ability to function properly, but many continued to display various types of nonconventional developmental delays. What was causing these impairments?

Medical journals ultimately became flooded with articles insisting that urban poverty was at the root of adverse outcomes, challenging the belief that drug-affected children were developmentally different from their peers. Despite these assertions, early childhood educators continued to complain about the distinctive behaviors of these children. According to teachers, drug-affected children were more disruptive, were unusually hyperactive, behaved impulsively, were easily frustrated, and showed delays in the areas of speech and language development.[23] Since many drug-exposed children continued to display various types of delays, researchers were pressed to learn more about the effects of the drug itself. At the same time, educational policy makers were trying to figure out how best to intervene.[24]

Toward the end of the 1990s, investigators set out to address the outstanding methodological issues in this area of research; they aimed to learn exactly what types of impairment were directly attributable to crack exposure. Studies were designed to specifically address concerns regarding the most debatable variables, such as polydrug use, environmental risk factors, maternal health, and the lack of adequate prenatal care. The results of these studies were unexpected, particularly to those who wanted to believe that crack-exposed children were similar to other developmentally delayed children. The findings continued to support assertions that the effects of crack exposure had been blown out of proportion. However, the results demonstrated that after controlling for these other variables, crack-exposed children continued to show some abnormalities, leading researchers back to attempting to study the drug in isolation. The severity of the impairments remains debatable; most studies have admitted that they vary according to the circumstances in each particular case. However, studies consistently demonstrated that these children are no doubt a higher-risk population.

The most widely cited study was conducted at Brown University School of Medicine in 1996 and funded by the National Institutes of Health.[25] Designed to control for the effects of polydrug use on newborns, the study assessed infant behavior using the NICU Network Neurobehavioral Scale, an instrument designed specifically for drug-exposed babies.[26] Infants included in the study were all full-term, were of appropriate gestational age, and had no medical problems. The design compared three samples of infants: one group included twenty babies exposed to cocaine and other substances including alcohol, marijuana, and tobacco; another set of seventeen was exposed only to alcohol, marijuana, and/or tobacco, but no cocaine; and twenty drug-free infants were a control group. The results showed that the cocaine-exposed infants showed increased tone and motor activity; more jerky movements, startles, tremors, back arching, and signs of central nervous and visual stress; and poor visual and auditory following.[27] The investigators concluded that although they doubted the drug causes extensive brain damage, prenatal crack exposure does produce excitable, stressed infants, even after controlling for the use of multiple substances.

Arendt, Angelopoulos, Salvator, and Singer, conducted another study to address the influence of environmental risk factors.[28] Focusing specifically on motor skills, the researchers selected a sample of 98 cocaine-exposed children and 101 nonexposed children from a socioeconomically challenged urban environment. The children returned to the hospital two years later and were assessed using the Peabody Developmental Motor Scales. The test examiners were blind to the drug exposure status of the children. The results revealed that the cocaine-exposed children performed significantly lower on both the fine and gross motor development indices; they had weaker eye use and hand coordination scores. The researchers concluded that when controlling for environmental circumstances, the deficiencies in drug-exposed infants are still evident.

A longitudinal investigation of the effects of prenatal care was published in *Pediatrics* in 1999.[29] The study included two groups of pregnant drug-abusing women—one with prenatal care (PC) and the other with no prenatal care (NPC). The women in both samples were of similar socioeconomic status; they were all single and low-income, and none had any education beyond high school. The PC women were interviewed about their drug usage at the end of each trimester. Data were collected from the NPC women at birth and during each trimester of their pregnancy. Nurses subsequently examined all the infants at the hospital. As in the environmental control study, the nurses were blind to the maternal substance abuse status of the babies. The results showed that the exposed babies in both samples had reduced gestational age and lower birth weight, were shorter in length, and had smaller head circumferences. The NPC cocaine-exposed group was significantly smaller than the PC nonexposed group. However, the babies in the PC and NPC samples had otherwise very similar outcomes.

Other studies published during the late 1990s demonstrated that drug exposure might have a greater impact on behavioral outcomes. These findings indicate that for whatever reason—the drug alone or other risk factors—most drug-exposed children will display neurobehavioral impairments that need attention. For instance, Richardson examined the physical, cognitive, and behavioral development of children prenatally exposed to cocaine during their first year of life and again at age three. The design used controlled for the other risk factors that impact the developmental outcomes of drug-exposed children. The results showed that the temperamental differences found in the exposed children at one year had increased to behavioral problems by three years. Most importantly, this study pointed out that these difficult problems are much harder to detect during infancy and early toddlerhood, which helps to explain why some studies have failed to discover these abnormalities in children.[30] Mayes and colleagues also conducted a longitudinal study of regulation and attention in 377 preschool-age children who had been prenatally exposed to drugs.[31] The findings revealed that the exposed sample had more behavior and performance disruptions than the nonexposed children. In various settings, the exposed children showed diminished responsiveness, decreased arousal, and increased impulsiveness. These problems, if not addressed, will develop into more serious educational problems down the line.

Currently Ira Chasnoff is conducting the most comprehensive longitudinal study to date of drug-exposed children for the National Association for Families and Addiction Research and Education (NAFARE), designed to follow children through their school years and provide information on their outcomes. A report of preliminary findings compared the developmental outcomes of ninety-five drug-exposed children between the ages of four and six to those of seventy-five nonexposed children.[32] Consistent with other research, the study found that cocaine had no direct impact on cognitive outcomes (IQ) of the exposed children. Although there were cognitive differences, the home environment was an intervening variable. However, the drug was directly linked to their behavioral characteristics. Cocaine-exposed children showed increased levels of aggression, delinquent behavior, attention problems, and social difficulties.

These studies draw attention to the need to develop more information on children born prenatally exposed to drugs, focusing particularly on the longitudinal outcomes. Some researchers claimed to have settled the debate, but the reality is that this area of research needs more investigation, particularly focusing on how these children progress through middle and high school. Clinical studies still have not determined the long-term implications of prenatal drug exposure. The follow-up research has made it easier for investigators to design more sophisticated studies on prenatal drug exposure and developmental outcomes; it has pointed out the importance of controlling for other important risk factors and has offered more rigorous research designs. However, measuring the effects of prenatal drug exposure has other methodological obstacles that are too complex to resolve.

For example, clinical studies are unable to determine if the frequency of drug use, the amount of the drug used, the drug's purity, or timing of use could impact children differently. Such information is important in determining if study findings on drug abuse habits are reliable. Data about drug use patterns are usually obtained through questionnaires, interviews, or surveys, which often result in inaccurate information.[33] It is very difficult for drug abusers to recall their exact use patterns while in treatment or the recovery phase, and it is even more complicated with populations who are actively using. As a result, data collected for studies on this topic are for the most part unreliable. More precise data about usage can be obtained through various laboratory tests.[34] Unfortunately, such assessments can only provide estimates of current use and cannot determine information regarding longer-term patterns of drug usage.[35]

Obtaining information about the severity of drug abuse is even more complicated with pregnant women. Many are in and out of the legal system, their participation in treatment programs is inconsistent, and most lack stable housing, making it difficult for researchers to gather the needed follow-up information, trace their drug use patterns, and retain them as subjects in research studies.[36] Although confidentiality is guaranteed to research study participants, the fear of punitive consequences prevents many women from providing truthful information. Studies have also shown that when women do volunteer information about their drug use habits, it is often inaccurate.[37] More than half of the mothers with positive cocaine toxicology deny drug use.[38] Therefore, although studies can gather some useful data on self-reported drug habits, they contribute little toward learning how these patterns may adversely impact the development of exposed babies.

The individual differences among pregnant drug-abusing women could have a significant impact on child outcomes. Factors such as the way substances are metabolized, the medical status of individual participants, the quality of prenatal health care received, and exposure to communicable diseases vary among participants and are known to have equal adverse affects on the developing fetus.[39] As a result, determining how these things independently impact how drug use during pregnancy affects the fetus is very difficult.

Although follow-up research has largely ruled out cognitive damage, one recently published study on the outcomes of drug-exposed babies demonstrates why these other factors continue to make it difficult to draw any definite conclusions on the topic and why the medical community has not reached any unanimous conclusions about how the drug itself impacts intellectual capabilities. In 2002 researchers from Case Western Reserve University in Cleveland reported the outcomes of a longitudinal cohort study of 415 children—218 cocaine-exposed and 197 nonexposed.[40] The sample was gathered from drug-abusing women who gave birth at an obstetric unit of a large urban hospital. This design also controlled for other risk factors such as polydrug use, caregiving environment, gestational age, and birth size. The investigators reported

> significant cognitive deficits, with the cocaine exposed children twice as likely to have cognitive delay throughout the first 2 years of life. The 13.7 rate of mental retardation is 4.89 times higher than that expected in the population at large, and the percentage of children with mild or greater delays requiring intervention was 38%, almost double the rate of the of the high risk non cocaine but poly drug-exposed comparison group.41

These children scored on average six points lower than the comparison group on the mental scale on the Bayley Scales of Infant Development. Additionally, the researchers found that the rates of clinically important developmentally delays doubled in the exposed group (13.7 percent) in comparison to the nonexposed group (7.1 percent), arguing for a clear-cut association between drug exposure and adverse outcomes. The study sample was gathered from a geographical area with a high concentration of drug abusers. The researchers were unable to determine if the potency of the drug used is the cause of cognitive abnormalities found in this population.

It is difficult to assess frequency of drug use, amount of drug used, or drug potency with existing techniques used to determine the presence of illicit substances in the human body. For example, urine samples are commonly used along with self-reported data. However, urine tests can only trace drug usage over a seventy-two-hour period, which in many cases is too short to be useful.[42] Furthermore, certain problems encountered while collecting urine specimens lower the testing sensitivity.[43] Hair samples have also been used as a means of determining drug use, but there are many problems with this method, including analysis, sample collection, and ethical issues.[44]

Gathering reliable data on prenatal substance exposure from drug-abusing women is not always a viable option. Investigators will often test the infants themselves to determine if prenatal exposure has occurred and to learn more about the effects of substance exposure during pregnancy (although these methods cannot provide the information needed to determine maternal drug use patterns). Urine testing is the most common test given to newborn babies. However, this technique has limitations in regard to the type of information that can be produced. For example, the detection of drug metabolites is dependent on when the mother last used drugs and whether the infant's urine was collected immediately after birth.[45] Inasmuch as women usually refrain from drug use for several days prior to delivery and investigators are often unable to collect urine samples immediately after birth, urine testing often produces negative results.[46]

As an alternative to hair samples and urine specimens, the meconium test was developed. This method analyzes the green stool that is formed in babies while in utero.[47] This first bowel movement is usually passed shortly after birth.[48] This method is useful to researchers because it can detect as late as three days after delivery the drugs that the mother used during pregnancy. The usefulness of meconium drug testing has been demonstrated in clinical studies of drug exposure in infants.[49] However, this test tells very little about the actual drug use patterns of their mothers, which is needed to determine if amount and timing of drug use have an impact on developmental outcomes.

Numerous clinical studies have been conducted on the effects of prenatal drug exposure—so many that it is impossible to cite them all. And though they provide an understanding of the challenges involved in determining the impact of prenatal crack exposure on developmental outcomes, clinical studies do little to address the educational needs of schoolchildren. However, they do highlight some important facts that educators must consider. One, although most drug-exposed children can demonstrate normal cognitive capabilities, for a combination of reasons many of these children do have developmental difficulties, which can become more problematic as they grow older and are expected to demonstrate more complex learning skills. Two, the self-regulatory problems prevalent in drug-exposed children will need special attention. Even if these children do have normal intellectual capabilities, problems such as attention and impulsiveness, if not appropriately addressed, will present obstacles to their ability to function in a classroom setting, also limiting their chances for academic success. Three, if attention is not given to the educational needs of drug-impacted children, many will fall through the cracks of the public school system.

Some Information on Schoolchildren

Although we know little about the educational experiences of drug-exposed children beyond preschool, some researchers have examined their outcomes during the early school years. Studies have shown that these children are indeed vulnerable to low achievement—they are more likely to be retained and are often identified for early childhood special education placement. Although not all of these studies are designed to rule out factors such as living conditions and other variables, and not all are based on longitudinal data, they have provided information on how drug exposure affects children's educational achievement. These results indicate that regardless of the root of the developmental difficulties found in drug-exposed children, it is important for public schools to become more active in addressing educational issues.

A 1998 study investigating the relationship between prenatal drug exposure and special education kindergarten placement demonstrated this point.[50] Outcome data were collected on 142 children enrolled in a Project Head Start early intervention program. Some had been exposed to drugs in utero, while others had not. The results showed that most of the children in the drug-exposed sample were identified as having speech and language problems and emotional and behavioral disorders, and 53 percent were subsequently referred for special education placement, compared to 29 percent of their nonexposed peers. The study also found that drug-exposed preschoolers had high incidences of medical problems, which could also impact their development and how well they progress through school.

Other studies examined teachers' ratings of drug-exposed children in the primary grades and reported similar findings. More importantly, these studies are consistent with recent research pointing to behavioral conditions as a major issue for children who were prenatally exposed to drugs. One study asked teachers to rate the behaviors of exposed and nonexposed children using the Conners' Teacher Rating Scales (CTRS) and another investigator-developed measure, the Problem Behavior Scale (PROBS 14).[51] Differing from the CTRS, the PROBS includes behavioral problems associated specifically with cocaine exposure. The teachers participating in the study were blind to the drug exposure status of the children. The cocaine-exposed group was rated as having more problem behaviors on both measures, demonstrating that these children could exhibit more-severe behavior problems as they grow older, making them more likely to receive special education referrals.

Also examining the long-term implications of school-age children, another study contacted over four hundred families to evaluate the behavioral outcomes of drug-exposed youngsters. The study focused on children born between 1989 and 1991, the height of the crack baby epidemic.[52] Teachers were asked to assess the behavior of the children using the Achenbach Teacher's Report Form. The results showed that the children who were prenatally exposed to cocaine had higher externalizing (aggressive/ deliquent) and internalizing (anxious/depressed, withdrawn, somatic complaints) behavioral characteristics. Such characteristics place these children at a higher risk for special education despite their academic capability.

We can also conclude that if these children do not receive appropriate interventions, they can become more problematic for the learning environment. For instance, Waller interviewed parents, foster parents, and teachers who have worked with drug-affected children without early interventions.[53] The interviews revealed that "as the children's ages increased, so did their anti-social and dangerous behavior—behavior that could pose difficulties for schools and society if nothing is done to correct it."[54] The younger children exhibited impulsive behavior, mood swings, and memory problems. Problems in older children had intensified to inappropriate social behavior and violent tendencies. We can conclude from all of these studies that early identification and subsequent intervention are critical to preparing these children for school.

Summary and Conclusions

Prenatal exposure to crack has been one of the most difficult topics to research. The debate about crack baby syndrome has lasted almost two decades, and still there is no overall medical consensus on this issue. Research studies on this topic have fallen into one of three categories. From the mid-1980s to the early 1990s researchers largely concluded that crack-exposed babies were a new biological underclass and that schools would be overwhelmed by the needs of these children. This wave of studies reported that these children had various abnormalities that would impede their learning abilities. During the mid- to late 1990s newer research began to challenge the results of earlier, less sophisticated studies on this topic, demonstrating that crack had not totally destroyed the cognitive abilities of exposed children. These new findings began to deconstruct commonly held assumptions about crack-exposed children and introduced other variables to the equation, such as unhealthy surroundings, the health conditions of pregnant drug-abusing women, and the use of multiple substances. Beginning in the late 1990s, more studies began to confirm that drug exposure could be directly linked to some of the impairments in prenatally exposed babies, particularly behavioral problems. During this period the challenges of researching this topic in the context of drug use patterns and individual differences between women became more apparent.

Although the research remains largely confusing, studies have demonstrated that many of these children will have educational difficulties and therefore need intervention. For the most part severe neurological or congenital deformities have been ruled out. However, these children frequently exhibit developmental delays. So far, we know that many of their problems will be in the area of self-regulation, attention, and speech and language disorders. We can conclude from all of these studies that early identification and subsequent intervention are critical to preparing these children for school. If we do not begin to pay more attention to this issue, drug-exposed children will end up in special education placements.

Lester, LaGasse, and Seifer provided the first systematic look at the impact this group of children will have on special education.[55] This analysis combined the results of the eight published articles on the effects of prenatal crack exposure in school-age children to estimate the overall effects of cocaine exposure on special education services. The results demonstrated that the average IQ difference between exposed children and nonexposed children is 3.26 points; although the number is small, it is statistically significant, and it means that a greater number of these children will be eligible for special education placement, ultimately increasing school districts' costs."[56] Based on the estimated number of drug-exposed births, the authors predicted a yearly increase of anywhere between 1,688 and 14,062 in the number of new students who will need special education services. Their analysis also predicted that between 4,000 and 30,000 more students would demonstrate expressive and receptive language problems.

But how do drug-exposed children fit in the scheme of early intervention and other special education services? The challenges of at-risk and developmental delay in the context of drug-exposed children are discussed in the next chapter.

CHAPTER 3

The Politics of At-Risk
Drug-Affected Children and Educational Policy

Introduction

One of the biggest challenges in addressing the developmental issues of drug-exposed children has been finding their place in the educational policy arena. As pointed out in the previous chapter, the link between drug exposure status and developmental adversities has been and still remains controversial. Although there was considerable attention given to serving drug-affected children in the context of educational programs, uncertainty about how the condition actually affects children created barriers to their eligibility for services under special education policy legislation. The amendments made to such policies during the 1990s drew attention to the complexities involved in defining *at-risk* as the term relates to children with nontraditional developmental impairments, particularly the drug-impacted population. Such policies were developed to address the new types of developmental problems and the growing need for special education among primary school students. The politics of at-risk in the context of funding services for crack babies also raised questions regarding which children should be entitled to services under special education legislation.

The educational policy dilemmas posed by drug-exposed children are detailed in this chapter. Explored are questions regarding educational interventions for drug-exposed children at risk for developmental delay, giving particular attention to examining how these children have or have not benefited from the services authorized under the Individuals with Disabilities Education Act (IDEA) and its the 1997 amendments concerning infants, toddlers, and preschoolers. Also discussed is how inadequate funding of special education intervention programs and the lack of knowledge regarding the actual needs of drug-impacted children are the primary reasons many have not had the advantage of participating in such programs.

Infants and Toddlers with Disabilities under the IDEA Amendments of 1997

During the early 1990s the drug-impacted population was beginning to enter the public school system. The influx of these youngsters was directly linked to growing special education enrollments in elementary schools. This problem was particularly noticeable in cities hit hardest by the crack epidemic. For example, the number of preschoolers referred for early childhood special education in Los Angeles and Miami had doubled betweeen 1989 and 1991.[1] Similarly, there was a 26 percent increase in the number of three-to-five-year-olds needing special education services in New York City.[2] These alarming statistics demonstrated the need to focus attention on drug-exposed children enrolling in the schools. Concern about addressing their adversities led some early childhood development professionals and educational policy makers to protest in their interest. Surprisingly, there were many obstacles to addressing the needs of the drug-exposed population in the context of children with special needs.

First, although teachers were noticing developmental difficulties among this group of children, research had not yet demonstrated how or if these children differed from other youngsters entering school with developmental delays—they were not mentally retarded or physically handicapped and had overall normal levels of cognitive functioning. This supported the belief that abnormalities detected in infancy would disappear by the time these children reached school age and that educational interventions used with other developmentally challenged students were also appropriate for the drug-exposed population. Second, the contradictory conclusions in research studies had not made the case for special educational policies and programs for school-age drug-impacted children. As discussed in the last chapter, researchers continued to disagree on the nature and severity of drug-related impairments, and some studies continued to suggest that there were probably none at all. Third and most important, prenatal drug exposure does not necessarily lead to a traditional early childhood disability. Although these children were demonstrating some educational difficulties, they did not fit into any of the usual special education diagnostic categories. Some were displaying attention deficits and other neurobehavioral problems, while others were also challenged by the circumstances of being reared in drug-impacted environments. However, existing educational policies and programs were not necessarily designed to deal with this group of children.

Nevertheless, educational policy makers were continually pressed to respond to the growing needs of young children with developmental challenges in general, and the drug-impacted population in particular. Too many children with developmental problems were enrolling in the public schools, contributing to the rising cost of early childhood special education programs. Educational policy makers embraced the need for more intensive programs for children with early childhood developmental difficulties.

Although the large body of research on prenatal drug exposure and developmental outcomes left many questions unanswered regarding their educational implications, two important facts about improving outcomes for children from high-risk families guided policy makers in responding to this issue. One was that early intervention is a necessary component to preventing early school failure. These services would be particularly relevant to children who were high-risk but did not have physical and mental disabilities. Second, interventions are most effective if provided as early as possible—preferably before children matriculate into school.

Under the belief that preventive intervention is the best solution for the escalating number of early childhood special education referrals, in 1997 a Senate-House conference made amendments to the Individuals with Disabilities Education Act (IDEA) to encourage intervention with high-risk children as soon as possible. Part C of the Public Law 105-17, Individuals with Disabilities Education Act Amendment of 1997 (also sometimes called the Infants and Toddlers with Disabilities Act) was designed to answer the "urgent and substantial need"

(1) to enhance the development of infants and toddlers with disabilities and minimize their potential for developmental delay;

(2) to reduce educational cost to our society, including our nation's schools, by minimizing the need for special education and related services when infants and toddlers reach school age

(3) to minimize the likelihood of institutionalization of individuals with disabilities and maximize their potential for independent living in society

(4) to enhance the capacity of families to meet the special needs of infants and toddlers with disabilities[3]

The programs were to offer social support and educational development services while assisting parents in cultivating the healthy growth and development of their children. States could also provide services to infants and toddlers who did not have cognitive and physical disabilities but were at risk for developmental delay if early intervention was not provided. This option would allow states to include a wider range of children. The law granted financial incentives to support states that would target these populations and encourage families to participate in the programs. The policy required states to address a set of fourteen minimum guidelines to ensure the successful implementation, institutionalization, and proper interagency support of the programs.[4] The basic requirements are as follows:

1. A definition of developmentally delayed
2. A timetable for services to all persons in need within the state
3. A comprehensive multidisciplinary evaluation of the needs of children with disabilities and their families
4. Individualized family service plan (IFSP) and service coordination services
5. A Child-Find and referral system
6. Public awareness
7. A central directory of services, resources, and development
8. A comprehensive system of personnel development
9. A single line of authority and a lead agency designated or established by the governor
10. A policy pertaining to contracting of making arrangements with local service providers
11. Procedures for timely reimbursement of funds
12. Procedural safeguards
13. Policies and procedures for personnel standards
14. A system for compiling data regarding early intervention programs[5]

The Infants and Toddlers with Disabilities Act was the first intervention program focusing on children under the age of three. Sections 671 and 672 of the legislation called for the development of statewide multidisciplinary intervention services for children and their families.[6] States were to coordinate interagency services for families. The start-up funds were only to cover the planning and coordination phase; state and local revenues were supposed to pay for the actual delivery of services.[7] However, most states lacked the resources necessary to fully implement infant and toddler services and keep them running.[8] The outside funding sources that could have supported these services had already been allocated to other programs. Furthermore, there were concerns regarding whether these resources should even be tapped into to support the infant and toddler services.[9] As a consequence, although some services were available, they were limited in their ability to provide effective interventions.

Financial constraints not only impacted the quality of services offered in infant and toddler programs but also had a major influence on how states determined which children would receive the services that were offered. The eligibility stipulations for the infant and toddler programs specifically mandated that states must provide services to children in the age range from zero to three who are "(i) experiencing developmental delays, as measured by appropriate diagnostic instruments and procedures in one or more of the areas of cognitive development, physical development, communication development, social or emotional development, an adaptive development; or (ii) has a diagnosed physical or mental condition which has a high probability of resulting in developmental delay."[10] This meant that some children, because of the nature of their disability, *had* to receive the services, and all other infants and toddlers *could* receive services but were not necessarily entitled.[11] Because medical research had not definitively linked prenatal drug exposure to traditional drug-exposed children (along with children affected by low birth weight, congenital infections, or environmental risk factors) were vulnerable to exclusion.[12]

As noted, the policy did say that "a state also may provide services, at its discretion, to at-risk infants and toddlers."[13] The criteria used for determining which at-risk children would be considered eligible for varied from state to state. Studies of the eligibility requirements for zero-to-three programs during the 1990s demonstrated that children who could have received services in one state were ineligible in others. Reports pointed out that some states used a test-based framework to determine which children were eligible. However, other states relied on other, non-test-based criteria such as professional judgment and documentation of developmental delay.[14] No criteria were developed to determine which drug-exposed babies were at the greatest risk for developmental delay and therefore eligible for services.

A major discussion developed around the issue of how nontraditional at-risk populations would be served under the new infant and toddler programs. The major issues were a lack of common understanding regarding what constitutes developmental delay in infants; determining which children in the at-risk category would be eligible for services; organizing a comprehensive system of personnel development, policies, and procedures; and developing personnel standards to meet the specific needs of developmentally challenged infants and toddlers. Providing effective services to these children involved new paradigms for early intervention services and new issues in the educational policy arena.

Speaking about the necessity to focus more on targeting families impacted by parental drug abuse, particularly these with children who had been prenatally exposed, a report was made to a House committee explaining:

> At the age they begin preschool, these children face a wide array of emotional and physical problems, most of which are only now beginning to be understood. Children exposed to crack cocaine in utero are known to be easily distracted, passive, and face a variety of visual perceptual problems and difficulties with fine motor skills. They often display problems with learning, concentration, hyper-irritability, and developmental delays.[15]

But most states lacked the appropriate resources to meet the needs of all high-risk children, including drug-exposed children. Though in theory the infants and toddlers policy was the ideal solution for responding to early childhood delays, in practice most states could focus only on children who *had* to have the services.[16] As a result, the number of states that initially expressed interest in programs for at-risk infants and toddlers declined 50 percent by 1992.[17] This was despite the fact that the need for such birth-to-three interventions was overwhelming. Congress allocated federal funding for the infant-toddler programs assuming that a smaller number of children would require the interventions. As the number of drug-exposed births continued to rise, more children than anticipated needed the services.[18]

In addition, states had the responsibility of demonstrating competencies in providing services to families that would participate in zero-to-three early intervention services.[19] Since HIV/AIDS-infected parents and their newborns and crack/polydrug-abusing women and their prenatally exposed babies represented nontraditional needs, early intervention providers needed to develop a knowledge base for working with these populations.[20] Some states invested in the necessary research, but most continued to rely on existing practices, which did not address the specific developmental issues with at-risk infants and toddlers. They reported having shortages of qualified personnel in essential areas such as speech and language therapy, physical therapy, and occupational therapy.[21] In addition, since the programs were designed to be family-focused, programs would have had to accumulate more information about issues pertaining to drug addiction and family systems and the issues particular to parents living with HIV/AIDS.

By the end of the 1990s states that had initially backed out of the responsibility of providing infant and toddler services under Part C of the amendments recommitted to the programs and worked toward full implementation.[22] The IDEA allowed all participating states a five- to seven-year period to institutionalize the programs and coordinate effective interagency services.[23] By the end of the five-year implementation phase, birth-to-three programs were in place nationally. Drug-exposed infants and toddlers are not necessarily benefiting from these programs, however. They were never included as a population that *had* to receive services. These children *could* be served under the at-risk category, but most states have opted not to extend services to this population. Only eight states and one territory—California, Indiana, Massachusetts, Hawaii, New Hampshire, New Mexico, North Carolina, West Virginia—have committed to serving this group of at-risk infants and toddlers through these programs.

At-risk children who are receiving services in these eight states, fall into one of two categories, both acknowledging the drug-impacted population.

For instance, the biological/medical risk category includes exposure to substances as a condition of established risk. The environmental risk category acknowledges that parental substance abuse is a circumstance that places children at risk and therefore these families are entitled to services.[25]

Class-action lawsuits were filed on behalf of children with developmental challenges but who were not receiving birth to three services. For example, in 1996 a federal judge ruled that the state of Illinois was failing to meet the needs of children at risk for early school failure. Nearly twenty-six thousand eligible infants and toddlers were not receiving the services they were entitled to under the Infants and Toddlers with Disabilities Act.[26] Although the law stipulates that eligible children are to begin receiving services forty-eight hours after birth, most were still being placed on long waiting lists—some for as much as a year or more. In addition, when children did enroll in these programs, they were not receiving services needed to prevent later developmental impairments down the line, such as physical, speech, and occupational therapies.[27]

Preschool Programs for Children with Disabilities

Early intervention services under the Infants and Toddlers with Disabilities Act were not the only arena in which the needs of drug-exposed children were an issue. Special education preschool programs had similar conflicts in regard to how children with nonconventional delays qualified for services under the IDEA. Many at-risk children were ineligible for such programs, leaving their developmental issues unaddressed before they entered school. Section 619, Part B of the IDEA dealt with children ages three to five and required states to classify children with one or more disabilities into a specific disability category listed by the IDEA. These specific categories included autism, deaf-blindness, emotional disturbance, hearing impairment, mental retardation, multiple disabilities, orthopedic impairment, other health impairment, specific learning disability, speech and language impairment, traumatic brain injury, and visual impairments.

By the 1992–93 school year, all states and other eligible jurisdictions had began preschool intervention programs for children with disabilities ages three to five and their families.[28] However, as was the case with the infant and toddler programs, not all were in compliance with IDEA regulations and expectations. Budget constraints and other operating circumstances continued to prevent many programs from providing appropriate services for all children with needs. Reports from the U. S. Census Bureau Survey of Income and Program Participation (SIPP) estimated that 851,000 children were experiencing developmental disabilities or had experienced circumstances that placed them at risk for developmental delay and therefore were in need of early intervention.[29] However, research on IDEA program enrollment shows that this figure is 30 percent larger than the actual number of children served under the IDEA.[30]

Most drug-exposed preschoolers needing early intervention services did not meet the classification requirements and were not allowed to enroll in the programs. Early childhood professionals were also concerned about classification issues more generally, particularly as they related to this population. Children had to be labeled as having one of the listed mental and physical disabilities in order to qualify for special education services. Since the adversities linked to prenatal drug exposure were not fully understood, drug-exposed children were vulnerable to being misclassified as having a more serious developmental condition. Advocates for at-risk preschoolers understood that in some cases this could be done with the intent of allowing these children to receive the necessary services. However, they argued that requiring children to be labeled under a category that does not fully represent their developmental problems might do more harm than good and that this would particularly impact children with nontraditional or more-complex developmental challenges. At the same time, although research had identified particular behavioral conditions as the result of prenatal drug exposure, many were challenging the idea that these children had permanent damage. As a report on the policies and practices of Part B of the IDEA explained:

> The research community was, and remains, concerned that in young children, some developmental domains are so interrelated—e.g., cognition and language—that the underlying disability may not be readily determined. The emphasis on assignment of a disability category in order to provide access to services may result in inappropriate diagnosis and services.[31]

Concerns regarding classification requirements drew attention to the limitations of the IDEA in serving at-risk students, drawing attention back to the need to be more responsive to those with nontraditional disabilities. Of particular concern was how to expand preschool special education services to serve the drug-impacted population. Their developmental issues were the well understood, and these children were among the most needy of at-risk students. However, researchers were still trying to learn exactly how drug exposure contributed to their developmental struggles and how these conditions could be addressed. Advocates for children with nontraditional disabilities discussed why the IDEA should amend the classification requirements to include those who are developmentally challenged but do not fit into any of the existing diagnostic categories. Giving particular attention to the drug-exposed population, they discussed the nature of these children's educational difficulties and explained why the IDEA should commit to broadening the range of preschool-age students who are entitled to services.

> [W]e as a society must realize that not only are the number of disabled children increasing but they are not those typically envisioned when the IDEA was enacted. Today's children are the victims of low birth weight, inadequate prenatal care and drug addicted parents. As a result, they may not appear to have traditional symptoms associated with disability. Instead they have slight neurological disorders which because of improved neonatal care do not necessarily result in losses of mobility or lack or coordination. These children, instead, experience learning difficulties caused by shorter attention spans, hyperactivity, or poor visual motor integration skills, rather than walking, talking, hearing, or seeing.[32]

With more attention being drawn to the fact that many children needing early intervention services fell outside traditional classifications, the ineligibility of children with nontraditional developmental problems for services became recognized as a flaw in special education policy. Furthermore, the intent of preschool intervention programs was to prevent the need for early childhood special education placement. Children with developmental delays who did not have mental and physical disabilities were the group who would benefit most from preschool interventions, which would reduce their need for special education services when they reached school age and thus decrease the overall cost to public schools.

In 1997 educational policy makers amended the classifications of the IDEA to address concerns regarding eligibility for children who were at high risk for developmental delays but who did not qualify for preschool services under the existing policy. As a remedy, a new category, developmental delays, was added to the IDEA classification criteria. This amendment gave programs the option to serve children under special education programs without the need to put them in a traditional disability category. This progress was spurred by the new challenges that young children with nontraditional disabilities brought to the schools during the 1990s and the fact that too many young children with correctible developmental impairments were being turned away from intervention programs offered under the IDEA or were being inappropriately classified as having a traditional developmental disability.

The new developmental delay category has been adopted by thirty-four states and Guam.[33] Although some have opted to use terms such as "significant developmental delay," "preschool delay," "preprimary impaired," and "preschool special needs," these categories are still intended to include children with nontraditional and/or hard-to-detect disabilities.[34]

Over time the United States Department of Education made a stronger financial commitment to early intervention programs under the IDEA. In

1987, when implementation of these programs first began, only $50 million was allocated by Congress to support birth-to-three services.[35] By fiscal year 2002 this amount had increased substantially, with $417 million appropriated to state agencies for early intervention programs under Part C legislation.[36] Part B programs (the preschool programs) also saw a significant boost in financial resources. In 1987 Congress allocated only $180 million for the three- to five-preschool intervention programs for children with disabilities.[37] By 2002 this amount had increased to $390 million.[38] States also secured additional funding through Medicaid programs to carry the cost of serving infants and children with disabilities.[39]

Special Education Services for School-Age Children

Justifying services for school-age children under special education policy legislation extended beyond disability classification issues and demonstrated that for the most part, society still resented the responsibility of drug-exposed children—more specifically, the children of crack mothers. Similar to earlier concerns regarding the impact that these children would have on health care facilities and social welfare programs, the rhetoric that drug-exposed children were retarded or otherwise severely neurologically damaged continued to stigmatize these children. More attention was being given to the rising cost of special education, particularly for elementary-school children. The very thought that "crack kids" were consuming most of the special education monies motivated parents to protest on behalf of their children who were already receiving services.[40]

The assumption was that the crack/polydrug-exposed population had permanent developmental difficulties and that special education funding was inappropriate to address these issues. This was true to the extent that programs were not necessarily designed to respond to their particular needs. However, the argument that such services were inappropriate because drug-exposed children had more debilitating conditions was misleading. These children did have developmental issues, but they did not have severe brain damage.

Questions were raised regarding the appropriateness of serving drug-exposed schoolchildren under the Individuals with Disabilities in Education Act. Opponents argued that these students would take opportunities away from the population for which the policy was originally intended—those with more conventional disabilities. Unlike the intervention services supported under the birth-to-three and special education preschool programs, schools were not given the option to extend at-risk services to school-age children with nontraditional issues.

For example, attention deficit disorder first appeared in the *Diagnostic and Statistical Manual of Mental Disorders* during the 1980s and is common among drug-exposed schoolchildren. However, there is no scientific test to measure this condition. For this reason the diagnoses made in schoolchildren are often challenged, with skeptics arguing that teachers are complaining about a condition that may not even exist.[41] Furthermore, when revisions were made to the IDEA, there was no information available on the outcomes of elementary-school children; had there been, it might have provided a direction for changes in policy. Only children with one of the more traditional educational disabilities could qualify for services. As a consequence, many drug-affected children are vulnerable to being mislabeled under special education programs, which have limited information on their actual needs and were not designed to respond to these issues.

Concerned about how drug-impacted children would benefit from special education resources, the National Association for Perinatal Addiction Research and Education (NAPARE) conducted a survey of school systems' definitions of *at-risk* during the early 1990s.[42] Only five of the fifty states had included maternal substance abuse as an eligibility criterion; eight were planning to include this condition but had not done so at the time of the survey; several other states had included this condition but with other stipulations; four states did not include maternal substance abuse as a condition for fundings and six did not address the needs of drug-impacted children in their draft definitions.[43] Teachers continued to point out the need to acknowledge this population of children. However, the politics involved in securing funding for crack babies forces most states to back off the issue.

School-District-Initiated Early Intervention
Programs for Drug-Exposed Children and Their Families

The issues regarding the drug-impacted population and special education funding were hard to resolve. Many children with developmental issues that needed to be addressed were enrolling in schools, and teachers continued to complain about the challenges of educating drug-impacted children. Several school districts in cities that had high numbers of drug-exposed births rose to the task and implemented their own early intervention programs to address the needs of the drug-impacted population. These programs target developmental impairments before children enter the school system and also offer comprehensive services to address the needs of the drug-abusing parent. Unlike the services provided under the IDEA, drug exposure status and developmental delay were the only criteria needed for eligibility.

For instance, the Los Angeles Unified School District started the PED program (Children Prenatally Exposed to Drugs), also known as the Slavin Special Education Program, for children between the ages of three and five. This program targeted drug-exposed children who had developmental delays but who continued to demonstrate normal abilities. Children with medical evidence of prenatal drug exposure, an IQ in the normal range, and behavioral characteristics and developmental delays associated with prenatal drug exposure were eligible to receive services.[44]

Similarly, the District of Columbia Public Schools created Project DAISY (Developing Appropriate Intervention Strategies for the Young Child) as one of the initiatives of the Early Childhood Programs Branch. This was a developmentally appropriate regular education program that specifically targeted children between the ages of three and five who had been prenatally exposed to drugs. Children participating in Project DAISY were integrated into small classes with nonexposed peers. The program used a multidisciplinary team that included social workers, a speech and language pathologist, a psychologist, and a nutritionist. In addition, Project DAISY incorporated a family support component to provide home-based interventions to families.[45]

The Ravenswood City School District in East Palo Alto, California, began the Parent-Child Intervention Program (PCIP) to address the specific needs of substance-exposed children. Working in unison with hospitals, clinics and child protective services, PCIP provided services to the families of infants, toddlers, and preschoolers. Parenting interventions consisted of education and employment services, child care, resources for substance abuse treatment, and other community resources. The overall purpose was to provide early intervention services for drug-exposed children as close to birth as possible. The Office of Substance Abuse and Prevention provided funding for this program.[46]

The Hillsborough County Public Schools in Tampa, Florida, also recognized the need for early intervention participation for children impacted by prenatal drug exposure. As a result, the Drug-Exposed Children's Committee (DECC) was formed. Acknowledging that environmental circumstances play a major role, school administrators, special education teachers, and community leaders formed a committee to track children between the ages of four and six for early intervention services. Through this collaborative effort, the district developed an in-service training program to prepare early childhood educators to work with at-risk children with different needs.[47]

Other independent early intervention programs were implemented to help drug-affected children make successful transitions to school.[48] For example, Head Start and the Robert Wood Johnson Foundation initiated a collaborative program to assist local Head Start programs in providing services for drug-affected families. These programs were also to provide educational services when the children entered school.[49] Family-focused, the program also linked parents to substance abuse treatment, social service resources, and medical care. However, the costly projects were funded by demonstration grants at only six Head Start sites and are no longer in existence.

All these programs were in great demand, as many children were determined to be ineligible for other services. Unfortunately, by the end of the decade, these programs were no longer offered. As was also true of many social policies initiated to address the problem of prenatal substance abuse during the late 1980s and the early 1990s, these programs were challenged by their inability to sustain ongoing financial support.

Expanding the Definition of At-Risk

Schoolteachers continued to complain about the problems with drug-exposed children and the need for intervention services. Ultimately, the IDEA expanded the range of services available to school-age children. Amendments were also made to address children with different types of problems. First, policy makers argued that the developmental delay category for preschoolers should be extended to include primary-school children, allowing them to become eligible for interventions. The president of the Council for Exceptional Children (CEC) testified before the Senate Committee on Labor and Human Resources concerning the reauthorization of the Individuals with Disabilities Education Act in 1997:

> CEC strongly supports legislative proposals to allow states the option of using the term "developmentally delay" for ages three through [nine], to allow children with disabilities to be served in the primary grades without the need for the diagnostic category. We believe that this option would allow services to children who are clearly eligible for special education but for whom it is difficult to pinpoint the specific disability at an early age.[50]

Drug-affected young children could benefit from the inclusion of the developmentally delayed category for two specific reasons. One, many of their subtle impairments are hard to detect at birth.[51] Such deficiencies become more noticeable as they approach school age. Those who may not have qualified for the birth-to-three or preschool programs could thus have the opportunity to receive services during their primary-school years. Two, the developmental delay alternative allows children to receive interventions without being classified into one of the traditional disability categories, which is likely to not only stigmatize the children but also make it difficult for them to move beyond this identity. Furthermore, inappropriate use of diagnostic disability classification labels contributes to misunderstandings about drug exposure and developmental outcomes.

The amendment reads as follows:

Children age 3 through 9 experiencing developmental delays.
The term child with a disability aged 3 through 9 may, at the discretion of State and LEA in accordance with §300.313, include a child—(1) Who is experiencing developmental delays, as defined by the State and as measured by appropriate diagnostic instruments and procedures, in one or more of the following areas: physical development, cognitive development, communication development, social or emotional development, or adaptive development; and (2) Who, by reason thereof, needsspecial education and related services.[52]

Allowing the option to serve school-age children under the new developmental delay category was a major accomplishment for the IDEA. However, drug-exposed children did not necessarily benefit from these changes. Decisions regarding which developmentally delayed children should be included in this category varied across states, allowing some to receive services and leaving others ineligible. Some states rely on quantitative results from standardized test measures of developmental abilities.[53] Forty-one states use a developmental test, thirty-six use a norm-referenced test, and eighteen use percentages, requiring children to have a 20 to 33 percent delay in one or more developmental areas to qualify for services.[54] In addition to quantitative test measurements, states also use informed consensus, informed clinical opinion, and professional judgment to help make eligibility decisions.[55] However, no uniform criteria exist for determining which children can be served under the developmental delay category. The drug-exposed population is largely overlooked because many have delays that are harder to detect using traditional assessments.

The 1997 amendments also incorporated provisions that would allow schools more autonomy in dealing with children who exhibit behavioral problems in the classroom. On one hand, these changes could be of benefit to drug-impacted children with behavioral issues; they allow for more children with behavior-related educational challenges to receive services supported by special education funding. On the other hand, these provisions make them more susceptible to being identified as also having more serious conditions and remaining in special education settings. For example, children with attention deficit disorder (ADD) or attention deficit hyperactivity disorder (ADHD) were made eligible for services under the other health impairment (OHI) category. The provision stipulates that not all children with ADD or ADHD would be eligible, however. To receive services under OHI, children with ADD or ADHD must meet two criteria: they must also fit into one of the other disability categories, which includes conditions such as autism, brain injury, and blindness; and they must need educational services as a result of that disability.[56] Therefore, to receive special education services, children needing interventions to address problems with ADD or ADHD are required to be classified as having other, more serious problems.

These changes were made with good intentions. However, very little attention was given to making sure that the drug-impacted population is specifically entitled to services and to learning how to effectively address the needs of children with nontraditional disabilities. Even if special education programs embraced drug-exposed children with developmental challenges, labeling them inappropriately in order to obtain services for them does little to help these children in the long run. For instance, as the number of young schoolchildren needing special education increased during the 1990s, funding to states to support the programs decreased. A new funding formula was implemented as part of the 1997 IDEA amendments. Funding for special education services shifted from using the categorical method to using an equalization formula. Under this new system, all states received the same amount of money for special education, regardless of each state's number of needy students. Additional funds were allowed only for children with more severe disabilities such as mental retardation. Research has shown that this has contributed to an overidentification of students as mentally retarded, particularly among populations who have historically been vulnerable to inappropriate special education placement, notably minorities.

The findings of the Harvard University Civil Rights Project further demonstrated this point. Explaining how children are labeled as having more severe disabilities to secure additional monies for special education programs, this study documented how school districts manipulated the system by overclassifying students as mentally retarded.[57] For instance, African-American students were overidentified in districts that allowed more funding for mentally retarded students. The study also reported that these students are less likely to receive adequate related educational services in those settings. In contrast, African-American students were less likely to be labeled as mentally retarded in states where funding was based on the general number of special education students and in states where funding is not linked to the type of services provided.[58]

Although the IDEA has improved the services available to at-risk students, early childhood educators continue to articulate the need for more preparation in working with these children, particularly the drug-exposed population.[59] This is an issue not only for preschool intervention programs but also in districts that practice full inclusion for children with developmental challenges. The Council for Exceptional Children also acknowledged that schools were having difficulty serving developmentally challenged children with nontraditional needs, particularly those children impacted by prenatal drug exposure. The council's report explains that although it has become acceptable to believe that traditional intervention strategies are appropriate, teachers and other educational professionals will need more guidance with these children. Urging that more attention be given to preparing schools for working with children with more diverse needs, particularly under IDEA programs, the report states:

> The problems we are facing are becoming more complex. Educators and parents who rely on the strategies of yesterday are not prepared for babies with HIV, who [were exposed] to crack, who survived childhood illness . . . or who are born very prematurely. The increased enrollment, increased complexity of childhood disabilities, and increased need for local taxes to be used on general education programs makes it imperative that the leadership, training, and research functions of these programs keep pace.60

A 2001 study outlined the challenges elementary-school principals face in meeting the inclusion requirements of the IDEA.[61] The findings support the need to give more attention to the different challenges of school-age children. The study pointed out that principals were willing to keep children with developmental challenges in the "least restrictive environment," as suggested by the IDEA. However, they expressed concern about the new types of disabilities they are seeing, particularly behavioral problems, and how schools lacked the knowledge to address these things. Principals explained that they needed resources to train teachers and appropriate support personnel. Therefore, these children are not likely to receive the appropriate intervention, regardless of the schools' level of commitment.

In May 2001 the Senate voted down a proposal that would have given states billions of dollars to improve deteriorating special education programs. This legislation would have provided districts with funds to serve all children with developmental challenges appropriately, allocating more than $12 billion for special education in 2002 alone.[62] Unfortunately, President Bush rejected such an increase and approved only $1 billion for special education in 2002, much lower than the actual cost to improve services.

In 2002 President Bush announced his budget request for the services mandated under the No Child Left Behind Act of 2001" (Public Law 107-110), explaining that this legislation is committing to improving the quality of education for the most disadvantaged children. Again, only $1 billion was allocated to the Title 1 program for traditionally disadvantaged students and the Individuals with Disabilities in Education Act.[63] The 1.9 percent increase allocated for Head Start programs in 2003 is only enough to maintain the current enrollment of about 915,000.[64] Children with early childhood developmental challenges need more federal attention, particularly the drug-impacted population. More funding will have to be put into improving the quality of their preschool and school experiences. If not, despite President Bush's promise, we will continue to see many more children left behind.

Summary and Conclusions

Most drug-exposed children will need preschool intervention to make a successful transition to school and to successfully make it through the educational system. The unsettled public school educational policy issues regarding the drug-affected population are not so much about whether these children have developmental delays as it is about how these children are different from other children with developmental challenges and how educators should respond to their needs. Several factors have contributed to the lack of policy and programs specifically for drug-affected children: (1) the contradictory conclusions in research studies on the effects of prenatal drug exposure on developmental outcomes; (2) the politics of at-risk in the context of providing services for children with nontraditional developmental disabilities, particularly crack babies; (3) the serious gaps in knowledge regarding how best to address the developmental issues particular to children born prenatally exposed to drugs; and (4) the significant underfunding of special education programs, particularly for school-age children.

Changes were made in special education policy to respond to the alarming increase in early childhood special education placements during the 1990s. Policies were developed to include infants, toddlers, and preschoolers at risk for early school failure. However, there are many loopholes in these policies that prevent these children from being entitled to the services.

Although these changes were not made exclusively for the drug-exposed population, these children were the motivation behind infant and toddler programs and special education preschool programs. Yet this population has had the most difficulty being served under this policy. Drug-exposed children themselves were never included in the circle of children who *had* to qualify for services. The IDEA expanded its eligibility criteria to include children with developmental disabilities that were not identified in the traditional categories. Unfortunately, there is a big gap between what policy dictates (theory) and what happens when programs are implemented (practice).

It has been almost two decades since drug-exposed children first became an educational concern. Yet their developmental needs have still not been adequately addressed. These children of poor urban drug-abusing women have been shortchanged from every angle. Their educational future has become marginalized in the larger struggles over early intervention services and policy.

The developmental challenges of school aged drug-impacted children needs to be explored. Questions about how drug-exposure impacts these children beyond the preschool and early primary years remain unanswered. Is special education placement necessary for those who still struggle with developmental impairments? If so, arc public school special education programs appropriate for responding to their needs? The policy and intervention needs of the school-age drug exposed child are explored in the next chapter.

CHAPTER 4

Identifying a Cracked Foundation
Teacher Observations

Introduction

Since the 1990s discourses about responding to the needs of different types of at-risk children, enrollment in special education has increased by 45 percent.[1] This figure is alarming inasmuch as only 11 percent of new students matriculated in U.S. schools.[2]

Drug-impacted children are one of the fastest-growing segments of at-risk students. These children were the focus of policy discussions throughout the 1990s and continue to influence public policy agenda regarding prenatal substance abuse among urban poor women. Yet we know very little about this population. What are their school experiences? How are their needs being addressed?

Too much emphasis has been placed on revisiting unsettled scientific debates about prenatal drug exposure and developmental outcomes. A public school perspective adds a new dimension to the literature; it examines the difficulties and needs of drug-impacted children in the context of what is happening to these children as they move through the educational system. From this perspective, the question is no longer the extent to which the drug itself impacts children, but how best to address their needs.

How are these children progressing through the educational system? Have their developmental impairments been overstated or understated? How do the symptoms of prenatal drug exposure impact their ability to thrive in a regular classroom setting? Are schools prepared to address their developmental difficulties? Has the social construction of "crack babies" influenced public school perceptions of these children? Focusing specifically on the school-age drug-impacted child, the aforementioned questions are explored in this chapter.

Epistemological Orientation

The epistemological orientation employed for this study represents a growing trend in educational research: placing value on the experiences and insights of teachers. In this paradigm, researchers gather information about important educational issues through the experiences of schoolteachers. Practical knowledge like this is best captured through qualitative inquiry.[3] Such a framework allows "us to talk about teachers as knowledgeable and knowing persons" about schools and school communities, teachers and teaching, and how children learn.[4]

Historically, research based on the experiences of teachers has been devalued and has had very little influence on policy decisions.[5] Information about educational issues is largely produced at the university professor/researcher level, overlooking the insights of the teacher/practitioner. In such instances, decisions are made according to the observations and interpretations of the outsider, ignoring the experiences of teachers who are on the front lines and can offer a better understanding of the issue. For this study, the teacher insights are treated as clinical observations. This information will help set an agenda for educationally oriented policy interventions for drug-impacted children with developmental challenges.

Research Questions

Focusing on school-age children, the following questions are discussed:

1. What happens to drug-affected children after they reach school age? Do their developmental impairments fade away?
2. Are drug-affected children different from other special-needs students? If so, how?
3. How have public schools responded to drug-affected children?
4. How can schools best address the needs of children from drug-impacted backgrounds?

Research Design

The approach used to explore these questions differs from other research studies of drug-affected children. This study used the mixed-methods triangulation design. Information was collected from questionnaires and semistructured interviews. The data collection instrument was divided into four sections: "Demographic Information," "Behavior and Learning Problems," "Teaching Drug-Exposed Children," and "Media Perceptions and Research Knowledge." Teachers were asked to respond to a set of twenty-five statements on the questionnaire, using a Likert-type scale. Teachers were also asked a series of open-ended questions. The information gathered will help to understand the public school experiences of drug-impacted children, the impact of psychosocial risk factors on their developmental progression, how these children are handled in the context of special education services and other developmentally challenged students, and, most importantly, public school perceptions of these children.

The Sample

A sample of teachers was interviewed from schools located in communities impacted by drug abuse. As qualitative methodologists have explained, this type of purposeful sampling technique utilizes smaller sample sizes and generates data from which "one can learn a great deal about the issues of central importance to the purpose of the inquiry."[6] The study sample was chosen from drug-impacted neighborhoods in cities where parental drug abuse is a major problem, contributing to high numbers of infants born prenatally exposed to illegal substances and children impacted by parental drug addiction.

Prenatal Substance Abuse in Three Urban Areas: Champaign, Illinois; Cook County, Illinois (Chicago); and Baltimore Maryland

Similar to other urban cities, Champaign Illinois; Cook County, Illinois and Baltimore Maryland have been struggling to combat problems relating to substance abuse since the mid-1980s. In addition to parental substance abuse, which has left many children lingering in foster care, prenatal substance exposure is an on-going social problem in these areas.

Including Champaign and Cook County, Illinois provides a small town vs. big urban perspective of the problem. For instance, Champaign is a small mid-western city located in central Illinois; Cook County, Illinois (which encompasses the city of Chicago, but includes other municipalities as well) is the sixth largest county in the state. This area has the greatest population density per square mile in the state and one of the worst substance abuse problems.[7] Eighty-one percent of all child abuse and neglect cases involving substance-affected births reported in the state of Illinois were in Cook County (predominantly Chicago), which is 71 percent of the overall state total.[8]

Prenatal substance abuse in Champaign has been a major concern in the city of champaign, seriously impacting the social service system in the entire county. Champaign County has the second highest number of young children in the foster care system in the state, behind Cook County.[9] Information on the actual numbers of drug-exposed children born in the city of Champaign and Cook County has been difficult to track. Although this work is unable to provide a breakdown of the specific geographic figures for Champaign and Cook County, the information available supports that prenatal substance exposure continues to be a pressing problem.

For example, the state of Illinois Adverse Pregnancy Outcome Reporting System, the Champaign Department of Public Health and the Illinois Division of Children and Family Services (DCFS) all provide conflicting figures. However, DCFS reported that between 1985 and 1998, the number of infants reported born prenatally exposed to drugs increased from 181 to 2071, and 90 percent of the cases were verified through subsequent DCFS investigation.[10]

According to DCFS reports, although the numbers in Illinois are still noticeably high, the number of reported cases slightly decreased toward the later part of the 1990s. This could be attributed to two things: one, the State of Illinois Adverse Pregnancy Reporting Outcome System pointed out that reporting of substance abuse cases is mandatory; however, testing of infants is not required. Since not all drug-exposed babies are tested, many cases are not reported to authorities. Two, the controversy surrounding the constitutionality of drug-testing pregnant woman during the mid-1990s is also a contributing factor. Protest against this practice influenced some public hospitals to slow down, or drop testing new-borns altogether. Therefore, it is impossible to get an exact figure for drug-exposed births in the city of Champaign and Cook County, Illinois.

Baltimore Maryland has one of the worst drug problems in the nation and the addiction rate in the city is double the national figure.[11] The city has sixty thousand drug-abusing citizens, which accounts for one in every eight adults.[12] One of the most devastating statistics of the drug problem in Baltimore is that in 1999 the city's drug overdose rate (324) exceeded the homicide figure (302).[13] Similar to drug-abusing parents in Champaign Illinois and Cook County, Illinois, many of the adult drug-abusers in Baltimore have dependent children or are expecting mothers. It is estimated that during the 1990s, four drug-exposed babies were born per day, which equaled 1 in every 10 live births.[14] A Baltimore Sun article entitled City Schools Must Tackle Special Ed focused on the increasing number of students placed in special education in Baltimore and identified drug-affected children as a major factor, stating" [O]ne reason Baltimore has so many children in special education is the ravages of urban poverty [including] crack babies."[15] The inclusion of observations from teachers in three different areas allows cross-references among the data providing greater reliability.

The Teacher Participants

Data collection began in the fall of 1999 and lasted through spring 2001. Six of the teachers were from Champaign, five were from Cook County, and five were from Baltimore. School principals recommended some participants. Others were referred by colleagues who believed their input would be valuable to this study. A few were identified by community members as teachers who could provide a useful understanding of the problem. Several learned about this study by word of mouth and volunteered to participate.

The participants also represent a variety of grade levels, classroom settings, and experiences. They are twelve elementary and 4 middle-school teachers. Seven have worked exclusively in regular education classrooms, while nine have experience working in regular education and full-inclusion settings. Two have worked exclusively in special education settings. Eleven are veteran teachers, bringing over twenty years of experience working in an urban public school classrooms to this study. (See Appendix B.) This tenure has allowed them to give a historical context to the problem and to discuss these children in comparison to traditional at-risk children.

Several of the teachers have close ties to the communities in which their schools are located, either living in the neighborhood or maintaining relationships with those in the community. This provides a valuable contact for their in-school observations and the community representation which helps validate their insights. All the teachers, whether they live in the neighborhood or not, are equally concerned about the educational plight of drug-affected children.

The public school contribution to conversation on this topic is long overdue. As one scholar writing on the topic stated, "little is known about the attitudes of public school teachers toward crack children."[16] Inner-city teachers have observed the impact of drug exposure on achievement outcomes. Theirs is the perspective of professionals who are actively involved in teaching these youngsters and who have observed their educational progression for over a decade. These teachers know more about the children's educational struggles than any other source. Their observations provide us an understanding of how and why so many of these children are failing in school. This information is key to filling an important void in the educational and social policy literature. The few studies focusing on the school-age population have relied on teacher rating scales and intelligence test measures of drug-exposed children. Such studies do not fully capture the challenges of school-age drug-affected children and offer no suggestions for addressing their needs. These missing insights are important to the literature on drug exposure and developmental outcomes.

Data Analysis

The data were analyzed using the constant comparative method, which is often used in qualitative studies in education.[17] As noted, qualitative data was collected through questionnaires and semistructured interviews. Analysis began with the first interview and was simultaneous and continual. Interviews were taped, transcribed, and organized according to the broader research questions. The responses on the questionnaire were cross-referenced with open-ended interview questions.

Three dominant themes emerged: (1) behavioral and learning problems, (2) psychosocial risk factors, and (3) the need for specialized interventions.

The Public School Perspective

Most teachers willing to discuss this issue were not current with the research on drug-exposed children. However, their observations contradict the belief that drug exposure does not lead to adverse outcomes. The teachers did not claim to be experts on the topic and admitted having no sure way of knowing if the problems are exclusively organically linked or environmentally exacerbated. Their observations are not based on the outcomes of clinical trials. Nor have they focused on discussing the methodological flaws in research studies. Yet they are certain that this group of youngsters is among the most vulnerable. These students brought new challenges to the classrooms, and teachers do not know how to best respond to their nontraditional needs. Pointing to the increase in parental substance abuse in the inner cities, particularly crack cocaine use among pregnant mothers in the communities surrounding the schools, they believe that many of the children's disabilities are linked to prenatal substance exposure.

A teacher in the Baltimore city school system has particularly observed the differences in young schoolchildren. After following the drug baby crisis stories during the 1990s, she became frustrated by too many articles suggesting that drug exposure has no effect on children. During that time, she was observing the developmental challenges of drug-exposed children who were just beginning to enroll in the schools. Interested in the long-term effects, she believes that school-age drug-exposed children have been forgotten by those who were initially concerned about their growth and development—a sentiment shared by most of the other teachers. She believes that the research pointing to poverty as the cause of these children's difficulties is the primary reason why schools have not addressed this issue, and she asserted that "public schools can tell a different story" from what follow-up studies have reported. Although rejecting the idea that all drug-exposed children are similarly impacted or that these children cannot be helped, she believes that drug exposure does have an influence on their educational experiences, ultimately leaving many labeled as having developmental disorders:

> I see a lot of the children in special [education classes] are from drug-addicted [parents], I think about fifteen years ago when crack was in the community and they were stating then that [the effects] were only the first few months— it's not long-term. I would like to see current studies on that because these are the children who are ADHD; these are the children with a lot of labels, emotional and mental problems, and chemical imbalances.

A teacher from Chicago with thirty years of experience working in urban public schools shared this observation:

> There were behavioral problems [with] children who came into the schools [several] years ago and the teachers knew that they were different . . . they had behavioral and emotional problems. I don't know for sure that it's crack, but these children are different. They don't know what's happening, but we assume it's drug exposure. We began to notice these children around 1990–1991, around that era.

The theme that children with multiple imbalances began matriculating in urban public schools during the 1990s was consistent across interviews. These teachers were fully aware of the possibility that public school perceptions could be influenced by stereotypes and so did not automatically believe what was being said in early news stories and research reports. However, they have come to believe strongly, based on classroom experience, that drug-impacted children do have early childhood developmental delays that become more profound as they move through the educational system. Still, although these children do have developmental challenges, teachers pointed out the crack baby stigma has poorly represented their abilities.

While the teachers believed that their observations were free from prejudices about crack babies, it was still important to probe deeper into the possibility that their observations could be influenced by stereotypes. To address this concern, at the beginning of each interview, special attention was given to learning just exactly how teachers knew the children they were discussing were drug-exposed, finding out how schools identified these children, and determing if (or why) teachers believed they could adequately identify this population.

Ways of Identifying Drug-Affected Children

Surprisingly, identifying extremely high-risk drug-affected children is not a priority for public schools. They have not implemented a system for tracking these children for early childhood interventions and have no educational programs designed to meet their needs. Although public health records, social service reports, and medical studies support the idea that these children do exist, information about the exact number enrolled in each particular school or school district is unknown. One teacher explained: "One year I might have four or five [drug-affected children] in my room. The next year I may only have one or two. We don't keep an official count, but they are here."

As a consequence, teachers have not been provided with information to assist them in finding out which children have been exposed; there are no assessment tools designed to detect the symptoms of prenatal drug exposure in schoolchildren. This is partly due to confidentiality issues, but public-school teachers know that this is important and are interested in knowing which children have been drug-exposed. Without the support of district-provided materials, they have learned to depend on a variety of formal and informal sources. Usually information they receive about prenatal drug exposure status is obtained through Division of Children and Family Service (DCFS) records and during intake interviews with caregivers. This information is helpful to teachers. However, this information is not always available on all children. Furthermore, hospitals do not test all babies. Therefore, even when these records are available, drug exposure status is not always included.

In addition, children from drug-impacted backgrounds change schools often, and initial intake information and social work summaries can be difficult to track down.[18] Therefore, even when drug exposure is suspected, teachers may have no sure way of knowing. As a result, some have learned to confirm their suspicions through other avenues. For example, a teacher in Champaign commented that her ties to the community have allowed her to use word of mouth to identify a lot of these children. She has developed a personal relationship with many of the neighborhood families and is "pretty confident" that she can identify every drug-affected child in her kindergarten class:

> I know a lot of the parents of the students coming in [to school]. A lot of our parents for kindergarten are under twenty. I know some of the family history, and [I know] that drugs has been part of it. Their parents used drugs while pregnant. Some are still struggling with this problem. That's another way of knowing who has been exposed.

Misunderstandings about Prenatal Drug Exposure and Young Schoolchildren

At times teachers' reliance on informal sources of knowledge raised the possibility that some of their perceptions could be socially constructed.

During discussions about the developmental problems detected in drug-affected children, teachers pointed out very specific developmental pat terns found in the drug-affected population that make these children different from other developmentally challenged youngsters. Interestingly, many of their observations were very similar to what has been found in research studies. This suggests that they were objectively observing the children instead of merely responding to socially constructed stereotypes.

They also explained that some of the common developmental delays found in nonexposed children may be mistaken as symptoms of prenatal drug exposure. Understanding how symptoms of prenatal drug exposure can be misunderstood makes it clear why it is necessary to have proper assessment tools for drug-exposed children and why school personnel should be trained in this specific area. It also supports the argument that for some children, the label "crack baby" could become a self-fulfilling prophecy. Therefore, identifying school-age children as drug-exposed on the basis of these specific delays alone could be a mistake.

Despite this concern, teachers remained confident that the drug-exposed population is not the same as the others. During interviews each teacher was asked to elaborate on the distinctive characteristics of drug-affected children. When discussing the similarities, some were more specific than others when explaining their observations. However, their responses were generally consistent. Their detailed descriptions helped dispel the notion that they were only echoing negative stereotypes.

Speech and language impairments were the most frequently cited example. This problem is prevalent among the drug-exposed population, but it is also commonly seen in nonexposed children when they first enroll in school. Therefore, as some teachers explained, this delay alone is not a reliable indicator. A Chicago teacher with thirty years of experience, nine years exclusively with special-needs children, stated: "A lot of children in early childhood special education placement have problems in this area." Although these impairments could have resulted from drug exposure, "it's very difficult to prove." Another teacher from Champaign shared this view. She believes that to label all the children delayed in this area as drug exposed would be irresponsible. Still, she admitted that almost all of the children that she knew for certain were drug-exposed displayed these impairments:

> You can't really say that all the children with speech and language [delays] are crack babies. I have children who need more help in that area. Since this is a full-inclusion school, children needing extra help are sent out for interventions. Children receiving help will usually catch up. But the drug-affected children are more delayed in that area. Some improve, but others don't. So I just don't want to say that all speech- and language-delayed children have been drug-exposed. But I'm almost certain that it is a problem area with [the drug-affected population].

Other frequently misunderstood characteristics are attention deficit disorder (ADD) and attention deficit hyperactivity disorder (ADHD). Most of the drug-affected children are challenged in this area. When discussing ADD/ADHD in young schoolchildren, the teachers emphasized that this condition is even more misunderstood than speech and language delays. Some of the "children labeled as hyperactive come from more stimulating home environments," which has led some teachers to think of them as ADD/ADHD, one teacher explained. Their early school experience is the first time these children have to function in a structured setting. In these cases, the condition is only situational and will usually improve as the child spends more time in the classroom. Thus it cannot be taken as a definitive indicator of drug exposure status.

The drug-affected child is "impulsive in a different way then the [average] ADHD kid," teachers asserted. During the late 1980s and early 1990s, "when the crack generation entered the schools," as one teacher said, teachers began to experience a different type of hyperactive child, one who could not be controlled with standard behavioral modification techniques. A kindergarten teacher from Champaign described the difference in ADD/ADHD in children impacted by prenatal drug exposure:

> Usually those kids are easily distracted. I mean above the norm I've seen them when they can't focus at all. Their eye contact is not there at all. They keep looking up at the ceiling, or constantly looking around. Usually those kids are jittery above the norm, I mean a lot of shaking of the hand movement, real impulsive kind of behavior. They're fine one minute, and the next they just go off the deep end. One of the severe cases I had, he was just all over the room. I mean he could not stay in one place. He always wanted to be under things, like hiding in a spot. You had to constantly coax him out of weird places in the room.

Teachers' ability to point out misconceptions about the common symptoms of prenatal drug exposure while discussing the specific problems detected in the children was encouraging, demonstrating that the teachers in this study have paid close attention to drug-affected children and have the experience to distinguish them from other developmentally delayed students. Their concern about not confusing these two groups of children was particularly impressive. It also demonstrates why it is necessary for schools and teachers to learn more about the distinguishing traits of the drug-affected population.

Distinguishing Drug-Affected Children

Speech and language delays and ADD/ADHD are problem areas for drug-affected children. However, it is important that they these two characteristics never be the sole basis for identifying a child as drug-exposed.

Teachers were given a list of problems commonly associated with prenatal drug exposure. The items were chosen after an extensive review of literature on the developmental adversities detected in the preschool population. Teachers were asked if they noticed the same problems in school-age children. Using a Likert-type scale, they were asked about their agreement with statements that drug-affected children

- are delayed in speech and language development
- have problems processing information
- lose control easily
- are easily distracted
- have difficulty staying on task
- have problems moving from one task to another

Teachers either agreed or strongly agreed with every item, demonstrating that many of these problems continue when children enroll in school; their developmental impairments did not fade away with time. Still, many of these problems can be found in youngsters with traditional disabilites. So what makes the drug-affected population different?

Teachers were asked to focus exclusively on the children they knew for sure were drug-exposed and give examples of behavioral and learning problems that are not common in the other children, linking these things specifically to the drug-exposed population. Teachers explained that although not all drug-affected children are impacted to the same degree, there are certain developmental patterns that make these children different from other developmentally delayed youngsters.

One pattern is an inconsistent cognitive level found in drug-exposed school-age children. Teachers have observed different levels of cognitive function at different times, which suggests that most of these children have the potential to develop properly but this is perplexing since many continue to function below expectations. Reflecting on this trait, one teacher explained, "It's like one day they get it, and the [next] day they don't." Some days teachers are certain that these children are special education material—they have problems grasping key learning concepts, and traditional classroom strategies do not make much of a difference. Other times, the same children will demonstrate some ability. This observation is key to understanding how drug-exposed children are often mislabeled as having other learning disabilities. Teachers offered no explanation for this inconsistency, but they were confident that this problem is particular to the drug-affected population and not a characteristic of other developmentally delayed children.

> Very short attention, having difficulty staying on task, the first two things I mentioned is typical with ADHD, but the fact that [the drug-exposed child]

can learn sometimes and sometimes they can't makes it different, which is not typical with the ADHD child.

One day they can do it, [but] tomorrow [they] never knew what we talked about the day before. In fact, several of the [drug-affected children], although they have demonstrated the ability, as they have gone on have actually been labeled learning-disabled in reading and learning-disabled in math.

This cognitive inconsistency helps to explain some of the contradictions in research about the impact of drug exposure on the developmental progression of children. As discussed in chapter 3, studies have proven that drug-exposed babies, particularly those affected by crack cocaine, can score within the normal range on intelligence test measures, yet they continue to display developmental difficulties. The teachers' observations support these claims. These inconsistencies present a major obstacle to reaching appropriate developmental levels overall, particularly for children who remain in school without any interventions.

Another distinctive trait of drug-exposed children is aggressive behavior. Teachers explained that drug-exposed children display "the physical behavior, the violent [type], other special needs children don't have." Teachers noted that these children have temper tantums for no apparent reason, at any given time, in any setting. Violent emotional outburst were observed by teachers in all three cities. Reflecting on one student in her Kindergarten class, a teacher from Champaign said:

It looked [as if] every afternoon at some particular time he would just snap. He would kick things, throw things [and] everything on the desk he would just kick off. Physically, we would just have to remove him from the classroom. It would take two people because by age five [they are] strong. He was so disruptive, I was a nervous wreck and so was my class . . . nothing set him off. He would just get frustrated.

A Chicago teacher described a similar situation with one of her students:

I've had some [who] were very violent, where they just go off the deep end. You have no warning. One minute [they are] fine. The next minute [they have] gone off. It's so disruptive for the class. You might have to deal with it because chairs might be flying. There is always the screaming and hollering. Sometimes it really disturbs the other kids.

A first-grade teacher from Baltimore explains why he believes that aggressive-violent behavior is the most distinguishing trait:

Normally, there is some emotional problem that is associated with the drug-affected child. They have more of an outburst, or a temper. Whereas a child with a learning disability just has a learning disability and nothing else.

These unusual mood swings have been identified as the major problem when working with these children in a regular classroom setting, which sometimes gives opponents an argument against keeping them in regular education classes.[19] Some teachers expressed their concern about how this trait can affect the educational experiences of other children.

As with the inconsistent cognitive patterns, teachers can offer no explanation for why this happens. And, like the unusual cognitive patterns, violent-aggressive behavior could be one problem that becomes more noticeable as these children enroll in school and are observed in a classroom setting.

Comparisons to Alcohol-Exposed Schoolchildren

It is important to discuss the differences observed between alcohol-exposed children and those who are drug-exposed. Although this study was focused on the drug-exposed population, teachers frequently offered references to alcohol-exposed children when making comparisons to other children with developmental challenges. Teachers who included alcohol-exposed children in the discussions were either exclusively special education teachers or have had experience working with children in special education settings. Their comparisons to alcohol-exposed children provide even more convincing evidence that teachers' interpretations can be viewed as clinical observations rather than stereotypes. Both groups of children have developmental issues; however, teachers believe that alcohol-exposed children have cognitive deficiencies that are quite different from those of the drug-exposed youngsters. As one teacher stated:

> Sometimes people look at all the developmental problems with the alcohol-exposed child and think that that is a drug-exposed baby, but it is not. These children have different issues.

Special attention is given to these comparisons for two reasons. First, these children were not mentioned on the questionnaire, nor were they a part of the interview questions. The participants volunteered this information in seven out of the sixteen teacher interviews. Second, the distinctions they made demonstrated why these children have needs that differ from those of other substance-exposed children and so should be studied separately. This also supports the recommendation that interventions be designed according to their specific needs.[20]

The alcohol-exposed children are more neurologically damaged and are more likely to need alternative education placement for mental impairments. Teachers explained that most of these children have a lower level of cognitive functioning in comparison to drug-exposed children. Many are labeled as mentally retarded. The chances of these children moving beyond that level are slim to none. ADD and speech and language impairments are also found with this population. However, teachers believe the drug-affected children are more likely to benefit from interventions and that this population is more likely to reach appropriate intellectual milestones. Some of the drug-exposed children who have participated in intervention programs have shown some improvements over time. This is less common with the alcohol-exposed children.

Also, there are physical characteristics that have helped teachers distinguish between the two populations. Teachers explained that drug-affected children can not be identified by physical abnormalities, whereas children suffering from fetal alcohol syndrome (FAS) have observable deformities. One teacher explained how "the fetal alcohol children a lot of times have the flattened nose" or some other "facial deformity." Another teacher concluded:

> As far as the learning process, I just think the alcohol baby is more deficient then the drug-exposed baby.

Another said:

> I had a child suffering from fetal alcohol syndrome. He didn't show as much aggression.

Research on the characteristics of children with FAS supports these observations. Children suffering from FAS have IQ scores ranging from mild to severely mentally retarded.[21] As discussed chapter 3, IQ studies on drug-affected children have shown that they do have stronger mental capabilities than alcohol-exposed children—their cognitive levels usually fall within the normal range. Research also supports the observation that fetal alcohol exposure can result in physical abnormalities. These children have an unusual head shape, low-set ears, a short upturned nose, a flat or missing upper lip, and a small midface and cheek area.[22]

Figure 1 summarizes the similarities and differences between drug-affected children and developmentally at-risk peers.

Teachers find it hard to place a label on developmental difficulties with drug-affected children and do not want to put these youngsters into any of

	Drug-Exposed Children	Other Developmental Delayed Children
Speech and language delays	X	X
ADD/ADHD	X	X
Aggression	X	
Inconsistent cognitive function learning patterns	X	
More likely to be mentally retarded		X
Physical Deformities		X

Fig. 1 Drug-Affected Children and Other Special-Needs Schoolchildren

the existing special needs categories. As one second-grade teacher stated: "All the children that I've had that I knew [for sure] were drug-exposed have had some sort of learning difficulty that is very difficult to pinpoint."

The Special Education Dilemma: Two Contrasting Opinions

[The appropriate class setting] depends on the child. As long as they are not a harm to others. The thing is, when they lose control, or [they have] mood swings, and they become aggressive, it's not safe for all children, but I think the influence is positive.

—Elementary School Teacher

I don't think they should [be placed in regular classrooms] because I don't think in a regular classroom their special needs can be met. They are different from the average ADHD [child], and they are different from the average student period, and so they require different approaches that they definitely won't get at all in regular education classrooms.

—Middle School Teacher

Teachers were asked their opinions on what educational setting would better accommodate the needs of drug-affected children—a general education classroom or special education placement. Most teachers believed that the severity of the child's needs should be the determining factor in this decision. Surprisingly, though, data analysis revealed that their decisions are more influenced by the age and grade level of the student. For instance, most of the elementary-school teachers were more optimistic about the positive impact of a regular education setting. General education classes, they believed, will provide drug-affected students with more of an opportunity to adjust socially. They also felt that the developmental delays found in these children are easier to address at this stage. More importantly, they believe that being in the classroom with other children prevents the negative "crack baby" and special education stigmas.

Overall, the elementary teachers did not believe that drug-affected children benefit from what special education presently has to offer. A major concern was that to remove these children from a regular setting too early would be a big mistake. Special education, as one primary teacher noted, "would probably do more harm than good."

I would say yeah on one hand, because they need to be around normal behavior—whatever that is. Sometimes we don't know that. Then again, I'm looking at all the disruptive behavior that causes other children not to learn.

This teacher's last statement highlights teachers' concern about the consequences for other students of integrating drug-exposed children into regular classrooms. Drug-affected children's tendency toward violent outbursts during class time can disrupt instruction for the entire class, which "is not fair to the others."

Another concern is the need for specialized academic attention, which also takes time away from other students. Although teachers are willing to accommodate drug-affected children in regular classrooms, addressing their specific needs is time-consuming. This can sometimes be overwhelming, particularly when there are too many students in a class. A second-grade teacher acknowledged that this contradicts her support for regular education placement. Although she believes strongly in placing children the least restrictive environment possible, she often modifies the curriculum to better suit some of the drug-affected children who are having trouble.

> A lot of the materials I'll have to adapt. I work in a full inclusion [setting]. If twenty problems are assigned to the other children, I will adapt to ten. If we have twenty-five spelling words, I will go to fifteen.

A teacher from Champaign said: "They are children who also need a lot of supervision," and "it is difficult for these children to keep up with the other students." So although those needing only an adaptive curriculum are better suited for full inclusion than those with behavioral issues, special settings still may be best for them. She further explained:

> They are high-needs kids that need a lot of individual help. When they are placed in a regular classroom and I have two [drug-affected] students who need my constant help, then I'm giving up time for the other students. They are so distracted that even though they know what to do, they don't go ahead and do it. So, they need someone to be with them a whole lot. A lot of time we classify our aid service into minutes and it never fits what the kid really needs. You may have some aide time, but it never seems to be enough, or at the right time. They cannot handle loose situations, like a lunch recess; it's just too open a situation for them. They need more guidance than others.

Despite these concerns, elementary school teachers continued to emphasize the positive aspects of keeping drug-affected children in regular education classes. They expressed both their optimism about the idea and concerns about the effect this could have on other children. In some schools these children will remain in general education, at least during the earlier primary years; "they are usually not placed in special education until around the fourth or fifth grade," one teacher explained. However, in other schools these children are referred for special education placement much earlier.

The middle-school teachers had drastically different opinions. They were less confident that the regular classroom environment would benefit this population at all. As one said, "these children have fallen too far behind" by the time they reach middle school. Their belief in the benefits of special education did not stem from a desire to keep these children isolated from the others; they were equally concerned about the possibility of public schools further stigmatizing these children. Rather, these teachers were motivated by the belief that special education classes, although not designed specifically for the drug-affected population, can be of some benefit. Middle-school teachers also explained that working with students at different developmental levels is more difficult at this stage. To them, the concept of full inclusion works better in the primary grades, and these teachers are better prepared to address diversity in learning styles with the younger population.

While discussing which setting would be more appropriate, some teachers spent time explaining the growing trend toward full inclusion. This has been one of the most debated aspects of American public school reform since the 1990s. As part of special education legislation, in full inclusion settings students with special needs spend most or all of their time in classrooms with their grade-equivalent peers.[23] Districts have adopted this philosophy in keeping with the federal mandate stipulating that, whenever possible, special education students are to be served in the least restrictive educational environment, and that public schools are to make every possible effort to keep special-needs students in general education classes. The law also stipulates that the students with more severe disabilities could remain in separate educational settings. Some districts, such as the Champaign County public schools, have already implemented this practice. The Baltimore and Chicago public schools are slowly moving in this direction; some schools in these districts have already started the practice.

Full inclusion is a good concept in theory, but teachers remarked that this system has shortcomings in meeting the needs of other developmentally challenged children and makes it even more difficult to give special attention to the drug-affected child. For this reason, some teachers feel that although full inclusion was designed with good intentions, until schools can provide better classroom support for teachers this practice inadvertently prevents developmentally delayed students from getting the extra attention they need.

Teachers focusing on this issue stressed that adequate classroom support is the biggest issue with full inclusion, they believe strongly in the concept because, as one teacher explained, "special education is such a negative label to place on students, especially the younger children." However, they insisted that if this practice is really going to make a difference, schools must do a better job of providing appropriate classroom assistance. Since many urban districts are strained for resources, obtaining the additional classroom support needed is often not an option. One teacher commented, "If you have help through an aide or if someone is there to do the legwork, then you can give time to working with [drug-affected children] or other children with developmental challenges. But, the support often isn't there." Another teacher said, "I strongly agree with [the idea of] full inclusion, but schools need to put more effort into making it work."

A teacher from Champaign discussed how in her district, special education students are sent out for services, then returned to the classroom with the other students. However, some children need more time to work on their problematic areas. This is particularly an issue with some of the drug-exposed children with self-regulatory problems. As already pointed out, drug exposure status is not a category that makes this population eligible for special services, and these children do not fit into any of the traditional disability categories. Teachers find it difficult to adequately help children who need more attention when the appropriate services are not available:

> If you have a teacher that has good strategies, you can show a child how to go through those processes a little more easier. When you have full inclusion and you have children on five different levels in a classroom, you have to find a way to move those fast kids along while at the same time addressing the need of that [drug-affected] child that may need more time.

A teacher from Baltimore said:

> Really, the system is not equipped to do full inclusion. Inclusion [in this system] says that there is supposed to be a special educator in every class with [regular education] classroom teachers. I have been teaching twenty-five years and I [haven't] had anyone in the classroom yet. The processes that they need to learn to help delayed children upgrade their skills, you don't have time for. The system doesn't give you the resources to do this. They tell you that you have to, but when you say, "Where is the special [education] teacher that is supposed to be in the classroom with me?" she is down the hall because you have a shortage of teachers.

Teachers are initially pretty positive about the potential educational future of drug-affected youngsters. However, as these children move through the system, that optimism begins to fade. Teachers begin to realize that if the developmental issues with drug-exposed children are not addressed early, these students fall behind as they grow older. Their mild developmental delays become long-term learning disabilities, and the minor behavioral problems become too much for the regular education classroom. The drug-affected population ultimately becomes mixed up with other developmentally delayed children. The fact that these children have the potential to develop normal cognitive abilities, despite their delays, becomes less important. More attention is placed on their developmental weaknesses, and their strengths are no longer discussed. Though traditional special education placement may not be the appropriate setting for the drug-exposed population, without information on how to best help these children this will continue to be the only public school option.

It was encouraging that despite the identified behavioral and learning problems, teachers still believed in the potential of these children. It is important to note that their observations are based directly on their classroom experiences. The conclusion that these children do have specific learning and behavioral problems that limit their chances for academic success and put them at extremely high risk for early school failure could only have come from public school teachers with extensive classroom experience.

No matter how much effort is put into determining whether the teachers' observations were influenced by stereotypes, there will always be the possibility that some of their perceptions were socially constructed. At the close of each interview, teachers were asked questions about research-based information regarding the cognitive capabilities of these children. Not many had knowledge about this area of research. Inasmuch as many of their observations are supported by findings in other research studies and was similar to the observations of teachers in other cities, this gives even more credibility to their observations. Other than the experience of their day-to day interactions with these children, the information most teachers received about drug exposed children came through news stories and documentaries focused on adverse development. Teachers recalled hearing negative things such as "the warnings [that] they just couldn't cut it . . . they were just out of control. It was nothing you could do for them. What a terrible situation." Others talked about "the buzz that they were just out of control. It was nothing you could do for them. What a terrible situation." Yet they still believed that drug-affected children could have a bright educational future if given special attention during their early years. Early intervention is extremely important to addressing the cognitive delays in drug-exposed schoolchildren. These interventions, teachers believe, are more effective if provided before these youngsters enroll in school. Children who have participated in a developmentally appropriate preschool program are more likely to make successful transitions to school and function at an appropriate level. Those who do not will have a much harder time catching up to their grade-equivalent peers.

Social Challenges Facing Schools: Expanding the Definition of the School-Age Drug-Affected Child

Our perspective on the school-age drug-affected child broadens when discussing the psychosocial risk factors. Most of the attention given to the impact of maternal drug addiction on developmental outcomes of children has largely focused on the prenatally exposed population. However, during interviews teachers pointed out that there is another group of schoolchildren affected by drug abuse—nonexposed children of drug-abusing parents. These children are equally vulnerable to school failure; they share the same psychosocial risk factors as their exposed peers, expanding our concept of the school-age drug-impacted child. When teachers discussed the social consequences of parental drug addiction, they noted that this situation is equally detrimental to both groups of youngsters.

Since the early 1990s, there has been an increase in the number of students needing school-based social support services. This problem has been largely attributed to the combination of parental drug addiction and poverty, which has deteriorated the quality of family life for many young children. Although many of these problems are traditionally issues for health and human service professionals to address, they are increasingly becoming issues that schools must also acknowledge and address. As a result, teachers have been paying more attention to the social problems that children bring to the classroom and how these interfere with their ability to effectively teach these students.

As a remedy, schools have hired more social workers to address the needs of children from troubled backgrounds. But, according to teachers, the existing services are not enough, and they are limited in terms of what scope of intervention they can provide to students. Most school social workers are limited not only in the types of services they can provide but also in their availability. Social workers are overwhelmed by the task of trying to meet the needs of so many students without having the necessary resources. In some schools there are no full-time social support services provided at all. Therefore, school social workers have little chance of improving the educational experiences of children from drug-impacted backgrounds. As one teacher stated, "These children have more intense needs." Because of this, teachers believe that more attention should be given to improving support services and hiring more social workers to deal with the growing needs of students. Also, teachers believe that specially trained counselors and psychologists are needed to work with these children and their families. Schools have worked to recruit more trained professionals, but most schools, for a combination of reasons, have not been able to meet this demand.

The issue of social problems with schoolchildren is not just limited to children from drug-impacted families. Teachers have pointed out that other youngsters from troubled backgrounds experience the same challenges. However, as is the case with the behavioral and learning challenges, these issues are more frequently found among the drug-impacted population. The most damaging problem is the lack of a stable home environment. Many children of drug-abusing parents are placed in foster care before they enroll in school. Some have been in out-of-home placements all their lives. Others have been shuttled between their biological parents and foster homes since birth. When they reach school age, many are still being moved around, and the average placement time gets shorter as these children remain in the system. Public-school teachers have observed this pattern in children from drug-abusing homes, noting that these youngsters could have four or more placement disruptions during their elementary-school years.

The impact of placement disruptions on academic achievement has been well documented. Since the 1970s, studies have shown that children in foster care are prone to underachievement.[24] Some have even concluded that these youngsters are more at risk than children of low socioeconomic status who remain with their biological parents.[25] Researchers have also reported that children who have experienced several placement disruptions are significantly behind control groups on measures of academic achievement and consistently score high on behavior disturbance measures.[26] The combination of drug exposure and multiple foster care placements places drug-affected children at a much higher risk.

Focusing on how the drug-affected population is disproportionately represented among public-school children in foster care, teachers discussed how changes in placements stunt healthy growth and development. Without a consistent caregiver, children cannot develop the emotional stability needed to be successful in school. These constant changes leave children feeling alienated from not only their biological parents "but their school family as well," as one teacher said. As a consequence, they are unable to establish bonded relationships with their teachers and withdraw socially from their peers. Teachers have also noticed that behavioral problems increase with each placement change. Particularly concerned about the emotional trauma of placement disruptions during the primary developmental stages, teachers discussed the multiple imbalances noted among these children.

> I have one [child] who has been in horrible multiple placements for the first six years of his life. He has severe behavioral problems that have impacted his learning. He is affected by drugs mentally physically, and socially.

> Most of the [drug-affected] children are in foster care. That is another component with not being in a stable home. They have problems bonding and it presents problems socially in school.
> A lot depends on what happens to them from the time they are born and the time they enroll in school. I had one girl in the first grade who had already had five placements. She has a lot of problems—more than the others.

Out-of-home placements are not the only cause of instability with schoolchildren from drug-impacted backgrounds. Youngsters who remain in the custody of their biological parents may also have multiple caregivers. When parents are deep into their addiction, children are often left in the care of relatives or friends. In addition, these children can be exposed to unhealthy surroundings by drug-abusing adults. As with children in foster care, these changes may happen several times during the course of a school year, which places enormous emotional stress on children. Such conditions make children unprepared to function in the learning environment; they are unable to concentrate and are bothered by their conditions at home. One teacher explains how such emotional unrest diminishes a child's ability to function properly in school:

> They worry about their parents a lot. The [children] in foster care want to see their [biological] parents and that brings on a lot of stress. The ones who live with their parents worry too. They are aware that Mom or Dad or both have a drug problem. Everybody in the neighborhood talks about it. Either way, these children are concerned about their parents. This is a lot for small children. So how do we expect them to come here to school, sit still, behave, and focus on schoolwork? It's unrealistic.

Some school-age children from drug-impacted families are lucky enough to be living in stable situations with relatives—grandparents or some other extended-family member. According to teachers, these children have fewer emotional issues. Although these youngsters do have other developmental challenges, they are more likely to improve as a result of consistent caregiving and nurturing. Relatives who are caregivers "know that these children have been exposed to drugs." Even when this information is not reflected in the school records, relatives who are caregivers willingly share this information with teachers; they are "very concerned about their education," one teacher said.

Teachers have noticed an unusually high transfer rate among drug-affected children. Frequent changes in schools inevitably result in disruptions in the academic track, causing these children to fall further behind. Teachers explained that during this process, academic records are often lost, preventing new schools from providing educational continuity, which is more critical during the early developmental stages. As one teacher noted, "It is more difficult to work through other developmental issues" when children are constantly changing schools.

Drug-impacted schoolchildren in unstable environments are also more prone to health-related problems. These issues magnify their other developmental problems and contribute to their problems adjusting at school. Many are already suffering from the long-term effects of low birth weight, inadequate prenatal care, and other biomedical conditions. Instability in the home environment prevents these children from receiving consistent medical attention. They are less likely to receive preventive care and are more susceptible to early childhood diseases and other serious health problems. A teacher from Baltimore commented:

> Some of these children have the worst health care problems that I have ever seen in elementary [students]. They are moved around so much that it is hard to keep up their medical needs. They need eyeglasses, they need to see a dentist,

they just need to consistently be under a doctor's care. As a teacher, I can only do but so much. I can't leave and take a child to the doctor. I can make a referral that a social worker looks into things. But when they are moved again, it's back to square one. A lot of times, their [health care needs] remain unmet. You are talking about their school experiences—this is something [that] adds to their problems.

Social problems become more challenging as children grow older and drugs continue to be a part of their identity. They begin to develop an awareness of how drugs have impacted themselves and their families. Naturally, at this stage the opinions of others become more important. Peer relations are more difficult when children become more self-conscious about being labeled as "crack babies" or a parent is known as one of the neighborhood drug addicts. Children are sometimes teased about these issues and made to feel like outcasts.

In some cases, particularly when there is a loss of custody, drug-abusing parents will come to the school to see their children. According to one teacher, "this is the only time some parents get to see their children." A school counselor from Baltimore explained how many of "their parents come to school ungroomed" for these visits. Ultimately, she says, "other students begin to notice and associate the child with the [drug-abusing] parent." Another teacher explained how this type of social embarrassment has led to anger in children of drug-abusing parents:

> These children are more sensitive in terms of their family. If you talk about their mom, they want to fight. They are more sensitive than children [from] nonabusing homes. Their parents embarrass them. These children live in a constant state of pain; they act out in violence.

Giving attention to psychosocial dynamics provides a more well-rounded view of the challenges of drug-affected schoolchildren. Teachers have explained why it is important to give proper attention to these non-school-related factors. It also demonstrates that the developmental dilemmas of drug impacted children are not just educational problems. Rather, they are school *and* community issues, and solutions will have to involve both of these social institutions.

It is important to note that all of the teacher participants were given the same questionnaire and interview questions, but each teacher elaborated on the aspects that he or she believed deserved more attention. Some focused more on the behavioral and learning delays. Teachers in this category had fewer years of teaching experience and found it more difficult to work with the drug-affected children in their classrooms. Yet they were no less positive about the capabilities of drug-affected children than the others.

In contrast, those placing more emphasis on the psychosocial dynamics believed that children's developmental difficulties are equally influenced by their environmental circumstances and that psychosocial factors deserve equal, if not more, attention. Teachers focusing more attention on the social risk factors shared four commonalities: (1) they were all veteran teachers; (2) they all had an overall understanding of the urban drug epidemic and its effects on the disorganization of communities and families; (3) they had a personal connection to the school's neighborhood; and (4) they all had extensive experience with teaching young children from traditionally disadvantaged backgrounds. For example, one teacher from Champaign shared how her close ties to the community and personal background give her a more in-depth understanding of the dilemmas confronting drug-impacted children. Her thirty years of experience in urban public schools has shaped the lens through which she examines the effects of parental drug addiction on schoolchildren. Explaining that education in inner cities has changed since drug addiction has become a problem in many neighborhoods, she discussed the complex interconnections between drugs, the community, and family life and how these affect educational experiences. "These children are angry," she said, because drugs have negatively affected every aspect of their lives—their families, their social life, and their educational development. Because of this, she insists, the school failure of drug-affected children should not be studied independently of these psychosocial factors. She spoke empathetically about how addiction has disorganized families:

> I'm a city kid. I was born in St. Louis, and raised in East St. Louis, which still is notorious for its [drug] reputation. I was around it, but it didn't affect me. I have more of a realistic view of what crack can do to your family and your kids. You have the remnants of what's left. You have moms trying to raise the family with no resources . . . or Mom has gone off and others [have gone off], and there is the grandmother with all the kids. . . . They're angry, one, because their body and their system cannot be controlled. And then they're angry because a lot of their parents are not a part of their lives, they're in foster care, or with Grandma, [and] Dad is in prison. That's what we see a lot of at our school, some kids with just attitudes. [Teachers] don't even understand what they are angry about. . . . I think they lose hope of being successful because of the way their problems are dealt with.

How Schools Have Addressed This Issue

> There are no programs [for] working with children who have had drug or alcohol exposure.
>
> —Administrator in the Office of Special Education,
> Champaign, Illinois, 2000

During the mid-1980s and early 1990s drug-related criminal activity infested many of the neighborhoods surrounding the schools. School and community leaders became concerned about the impact of this environment on the children. In response, many prevention and intervention programs were implemented. These programs aimed to free school neighborhoods from drug-influenced crime and keep children away from drug-related activity. The specific goals were to prevent drug-related gang activities, control violence in the schools, and decrease drug activity in the school neighborhood. Two of the most popular approaches, Drug Abuse Resistance Education (DARE) and the Safe and Drug-Free School program, have been implemented in school districts across the country.

Schools have also worked to address the problem of substance abuse among students. Substance abuse education programs have been incorporated into the curriculum in many districts. These programs provide training for teachers and other school staff to help them encourage children to stay away from drugs. School-based drug-counseling and referral resources have also been implemented in many middle and high schools. Some districts have even implemented tough punitive policies on student substance abuse. Teachers interviewed for this study discussed the different drug intervention programs and wondered if schools will ever address the most pressing problem—school failure of children from drug-impacted backgrounds, particularly the ones who have been prenatally exposed.

Teachers are turned off by the fact that there is so much research on improving the educational outcomes of at-risk populations, yet schools rarely see any results in the most vulnerable children. As one teacher said, "[There is] so much research going on in schools in poor neighborhoods. But how do [these studies] actually help the kids?" Perplexed about how little attention has been given to children from drug-impacted backgrounds, she shared her concerns about researchers coming into schools. Normally, her voluntary participation and cooperation in research studies is rare. Her decision to participate in this study was motivated by her concern for the educational plight of drug-affected children and her appreciation of someone who valued the opinions of public school teachers.

> Do [researchers] really care about what is going on with drug-affected children? Why is it that someone is just coming in to talk to us about drug-affected children? Maybe this is why they don't know what's going on with these kids. I can tell you what happens to them when they come to school. Most of them fail because schools don't know what to do with these children.

Teachers also voiced their dissatisfaction with in-services on prenatal drug exposure and developmental outcomes. Schools attempted to address this problem during the early 1990s by providing teachers with information about drug-exposed infants, particularly crack babies. Workshops gave teachers information about the epidemiology of prenatal drug exposure, the statistics demonstrating the escalation in the number of drug-exposed children born to poor inner-city women, and the projected problems that inner-city schools could face. But teachers received very little information about how to address the educational challenges of these children: "nothing to help teachers in the classroom."

At the conclusion of an interview, one teacher remarked, "You are doing the research; now you have to tell us what to do with them." A teacher from Champaign summed up the general sentiment among teachers regarding research and drug-affected children in her school:

> Teachers get turned off because a lot of times when they bring people in, we get the statistics. I don't need the statistics. I know what the kids do, I look at them every day in the room. I want to know how to deal with these kids. So if you're going to come in and talk to me, I don't want to hear all the statistics. A little statistics is great, but I want to know how to deal with these kids, and I think that's where the teachers get turned off. We don't get help, we get more literature. I can write a book about what the kids are doing. I want some concrete strategies to use.

A teacher from Baltimore echoed these feelings:

> I have been a classroom teacher for thirty-one years [and] I have never had anyone, never in any of the districts that I have taught in—New Jersey, New York, Pennsylvania, or here in Baltimore, Maryland—[say], "Here is what you do."

A teacher from Chicago wants to know more about how to address the needs of drug-affected children in her classroom:

> I wish we knew more about how to teach them. They would probably be okay. But we don't understand enough. It's a waste of time trying to figure out what's wrong with a student and trying to provide them with the correct kinds of services if we don't know what we [are] looking for.

The lack of guidance from university special education programs has also been disappointing. Teachers are surprised to learn that these programs have not given adequate attention to the drug-affected population. The newer teachers explained that in programs that have addressed the topic, there is not enough research on the school-age population to prepare teachers to work with these children. They acknowledge that the number of high-risk elementary-school children is growing and that their needs are much more complex. However, there is nothing dealing specifically with how to teach drug-exposed children with nontraditional disabilities. In these programs, as one teacher explained, "they just touch on the subject, but they really don't tell you much." Veteran teachers attributed this to the fact that this is a fairly new educational topic. Noted one interviewee, "[The crack baby] just wasn't around when I was in school."

According to the veteran teachers, "experience has been the best teacher" for learning how to deal with these children. Over time they have learned how to better cope with drug-affected children, but they say they still need educational programs or interventions to address these children's specific needs. One teacher expressed sympathy for less experienced teachers who are having a harder time coping with these students: "I don't know how I would react these days as a new teacher."

Working with Drug-Affected Children

The teachers participating in this study hope that public education will begin to focus on the special needs of the drug-affected population. However, they did not seem very confident that this will happen. Schools already have a difficult time responding to other learner diversity needs, and "crack babies [are] just a controversial topic and no one wants to deal with this issue." Although the teachers participating in this study have an optimistic attitude about drug-affected children, they admit that this outlook is not shared by all of their colleagues. Some explained that other teachers are less willing to put effort into working with these children, even during the elementary school years. This is largely attributed to their lack of information on the developmental potential of school-age children, which has led many to believe some of the negative stereotypes, such as that they are a biological underclass, that some of these children have permanent brain damage, that their problems cannot be helped, and that they will only drain resources from other children. These attitudes, teachers say, will ultimately influence how schools respond to this issue in the future.

Speaking about the negative attitudes, one teacher commented: "Some teachers believe [drug-affected children] cannot be helped and give up on them." Another noted how some "teachers just cannot get past their behavior and look at what they can do. [Some teachers] are so stuck in [the belief] that they are bad kids and won't cooperate. That's all they look at." Discussing how trends in alternative education placements are moving toward including younger children, a teacher from Champaign expressed the opinion that this will impact the educational futures of drug-affected children with developmental delays. The growing number of problem children has influenced changes in alternative education in that district, and she believes that negative teacher attitudes are directly linked to the movement toward more alternative school placement options. She spoke about the Care School, which is an alternative high school:

> By high school you're out. In Champaign you go to the Care School. They have Care Middle [School] now, but teachers are saying: "When are you going to get one for elementary?"[27]

Teachers interviewed for this book were clear that schools have not made the educational needs of drug-affected children a priority. The main purpose of this study is to learn more about the educational experiences of drug-impacted schoolchildren and to offer suggestions to shape educational policies and programs. Although this is not a teacher method book about working with drug-exposed children, teachers shared their opinions about how schools should intervene and what classroom strategies have made some difference. Most of the study participants have admitted to not knowing exactly what will make a difference in long-term outcomes. But they have years of valuable experience and believe that some of their insights will benefit others.

> When you have worked with young children for almost 30 years, you learn a lot about different learning styles. I don't know how much of a difference these will make in the long term. But this is what I have learned to do in my class and it helps. Sometimes these things can make the difference between a good or a bad day. The behavioral issues make teaching them are more difficult to deal with. But I do believe that you can work with some of the learning problems.

Although teachers offered their suggestions for classroom strategies, they continued to stress the need for research-based information to guide them in working with these students. Many of their suggestions are similar to the techniques used in specially designed preschool programs, which supports the value of their classroom experiences and observations in regard to the developmental issues of drug-exposed children.

The teachers who discussed this topic focused on three main things: teacher attitude, pedagogical style, and individual attention and small class size.

Attitude

When discussing effective strategies, teachers continued to focus on the power of positive attitudes. Attitude, teachers explained, is the most important factor in teaching children from high-risk environments. This is even more important when teaching drug-affected children because of the stigma placed on drug-exposed babies in inner cities and the initial projected outcomes for this population. They explained how "when you have bought into the stereotypes" about crack babies, "you really don't give them a chance to be successful." Teachers may have to use different strategies, but it is important that these children "are not treated differently from the other children in the class." Another elaborates:

> I know [drug-exposed children] have problems. But I still have to work with them and believe that they can improve. Some of these children are actually smart. They just have other [issues] and it keeps them from working to their potential. I still remain positive and hope that what I can't make better, the next teacher will. If they get [a teacher] with a messed-up attitude, these children will definitely fail. Don't get me wrong—some of these children have

some serious problems that a [positive attitude] can't make better. I just believe that teacher attitude makes a big difference for these students.

Pedagogical Style

Drug-affected children learn better in atmospheres that complement their behavioral style. Teachers discourage passive learning exercises with these children. This is largely attributed to their hyperactivity and short attention spans. This condition makes it difficult for these children to work by themselves or to be less than totally involved in the learning process. Although active learning exercises may work, teachers explained, these children also need routine and predictability. A highly structured environment, they believe, is absolutely necessary for a hyperactive, drug-affected child. Teachers also explained that these children need "lots of cues to stay on task," and "they learn better by visual things rather than hearing."

Classroom Strategies

Below is a list of the instructional practices that veteran elementary school teachers have found to have some impact with drug-affected children. Such allow drug-affected children to demonstrate their abilities, in spite of their challenges.

- Teach using lots of verbal cues
- Use lots of audio and visual aids
- Use lots of repetition
- Incorporate behavioral modification charts with rewards and consequences
- Employ lots of hands-on activities

Individual Attention and Small Class Size

For the strategies listed above to work, teachers believe, these children have to be in smaller classes. As mentioned earlier, when these children are in larger general education classes, teachers are unable to give them more focused attention. Also it takes more time to prepare assignments for drug-exposed children.

According to some teachers, providing separate classes for drug-affected children who need more specialized attention is "better than special ed." One teacher explained that since drug exposure affects children in different ways, "the ones who will benefit from a specially designed curriculum should spend [some] time in a separate class," but not special education. One teacher offered the opinion that separating these children temporarily is a good way of "addressing their need for individual attention." Another teacher who agreed with this suggestion added that this "may not be as helpful to the ones who are more damaged." She noted that one intervention would not work for all, as these children can have drastically different needs:

> I've seen very smart students who are crack babies. Once they have had proper medication to control their mood swings and attention span, they do fine. They will just need some help with their other problems. I believe that intervention will make a big difference. And I've seen the opposite. Their brain just doesn't function like a normal kid and they can't process the information.

The suggestions offered address the most correctable problems—short attention spans, hyperactivity, and the different learning style of drug-affected children. More individual attention, a responsive teaching style, and appropriate classroom activities can help make their classroom experiences more positive. Teachers admitted, however, that they are not sure how to respond to these children's unusual behavior and inconsistent cognitive patterns. Teachers believe that these are issues for other professionals to address. The more optimistic view is that with intervention during their early years, most of these children will outgrow their cognitive inconsistencies. The more realistic view is that many will continue to move through the system without having the advantage of interventions.

Summary and Conclusions

Teachers agreed on several points:

- Schools have no assessment tools for detecting the symptoms of prenatal drug exposure.
- The developmental impairments detected in most drug-affected preschool-age children continue when they reach school age.
- Speech and language delays and ADD/ADHD are generally misinterpreted as symptoms of drug exposure in other developmentally delayed youngsters.
- Although the drug-affected population shares some characteristics with other developmentally delayed children, they also have differences. Their inconsistent cognitive levels and behavioral patterns are some distinguishing traits.
- Nonexposed children of drug-abusing parents are equally vulnerable to school failure.
- As these children grow older without the support of interventions, teachers lose hope that their needs can be addressed.
- Educational interventions must address the psychosocial risk factors.
- Schools need guidance in responding to the needs of children impacted by parental substance abuse.

Many drug-exposed children are coming to school unprepared for the learning environment. The most significant finding of this study is that schools have still not invested in learning how to work with these children through educational interventions. With the exception of specially designed early intervention programs implemented during the early 1990s, schools have not provided teachers with information about best classroom practices for drug-exposed schoolchildren. As a result, these youngsters have been dumped into public schools where neither regular education, full inclusion, nor special education classrooms are designed to address their developmental difficulties.

This study provides an understanding of the challenges involved with teaching school-age drug-affected children. The information gathered on their learning and behavioral problems, such as hyperactivity, attention deficit, and speech and language impairments, is not new; research has already documented these problems in toddlers and preschool children. The public school perspective has contributed to the literature by explaining how these specific behavioral and learning problems play out in a classroom setting, placing these children in a unique high-risk category—many ending up in public school special education programs, which do little to address their problems.

More longitudinal studies following specific schoolchildren over an extended period are extremely important to determine the actual long-term effects of prenatal drug exposure. This would give a good idea of how many have actually outgrown the symptoms and are progressing well, how many children continue to display developmental delays, how many end up in special education classes or alternative school settings, how many are labeled mentally retarded or put into other special-needs categories, and how many stay in school or drop out. This study was initially designed to include such information. However, there were many confidentiality and ethics issues that prevented schools from disclosing information in student files. Furthermore, as pointed out earlier, information on prenatal drug exposure is derived from various sources, and schools have not started to systematically collect this information. However, that does not take away from the value of the teachers' insights and the overall implications of this study.

This qualitative study provides a more in-depth understanding of what is happening to drug-exposed schoolchildren. As pointed out, quantitive studies cannot provide this kind of information or fully explain their classroom dilemmas. The teachers' insights demonstrate why public schools must begin to pay more attention to this issue, and how and why some of these children, although capable, are doomed to failure.

Future studies must also focus more on studying drug-impacted children in an educational context. This means that education professionals must leave the methodological debates to the scientific researchers. Revisiting these arguments will not take this research in the direction that helps children. It will only continue to marginalize their critical need for educational interventions. Additionally, we must pay far less attention to the damaging stereotypes of drug-affected children. There is no doubt that they are academically fragile and will need special attention, but extensive research has already made it clear that the crack baby stigma does make these children susceptible to stereotypes. Our main focus as educators must be on learning more about the real impact of prenatal drug exposure and providing better educational experiences for schoolchildren.

This study not only has implications for the drug-exposed population but also demonstrates that public education must begin to seriously respond to the needs of children who enter school with developmental challenges but are capable of normal intellectual functioning. These inappropriate labeled children make up most of the public school special education students. These settings are not addressing their developmental difficulties; rather, they are contributing to the children's low educational achievement. For instance, one study found that undeveloped reading skills are a major reason for special education placement.[28] However, when children are placed in special education settings, they do less reading than when they are in regular education classrooms.[29] Therefore, these programs are not equipped to bring any of the children with early childhood delays up to grade level. Many special education teachers in urban school systems lack the appropriate training, and programs are failing to respond to the call for more appropriate services.[30] It is of extreme importance that public education begin to implement more appropriate services for at-risk schoolchildren—this is an unresolved issue of the educational issues of the 1990s. Too many students are moving through the system with their needs unaddressed. If those needs are not addressed in this decade, we will continue to see many bright students fail in substandard school-based special education programs.

CHAPTER 5

Healing the Crack in Their World

Education and Drug-Affected Children

Introduction

Drug-impacted children would clearly benefit from programs designed to address their specific developmental challenges. Policies must be developed to address the risk factors that also impact their educational experiences, which means not only targeting their specific behavioral and learning problems but also addressing the psychosocial risk factors that are common with children from drug-impacted backgrounds. Such interventions will have to be approached from a multidisciplinary perspective and designed to begin before these children enroll in school. This means bridging the gaps among education, public health, human services, and addiction treatment programs focused on pregnant women and mothers with very young children.

This chapter offers suggestions for creating educational and social programs aimed specifically at preventing early school failure in children impacted by parental drug abuse in general and prenatal substance exposure in particular. Beginning with the early intervention process, this section places the developmental needs of drug-impacted children at the center of the discussion regarding prenatal substance abuse. Most importantly, this discussion demonstrates why efforts to seriously address prenatal drug abuse must make this aspect of the problem an important part of the social policy agenda and advocate for adequate funding for related educational and social programs.

The second half of the chapter explores educational interventions for school-age children. Focusing on the limitations of special education programs in regard to meeting the needs of the drug-impacted population, this section explains why these children should not be labeled according to conventional early childhood disability classifications and makes the case for public education to begin advocating on their behalf. This discussion also has implications for developing school and community partnerships and incorporating effective classroom intervention strategies. Finally, it addresses the special education policy dilemma in relation to drug-exposed schoolchildren with developmental challenges.

Early Intervention and Drug-Impacted Families: Implications for Health, Human Services, and Educational Policy

Policy makers will need to focus more attention on addressing the needs of drug-abusing women and their children. This is particularly important as addiction continues to be a problem among women of childbearing age. In 2001, the Substance Abuse and Mental Health Services Administration reported that at the end of the 1990s the percentage of this population involved with drugs, particularly crack cocaine, was rising.[1] Most disturbing, the percentage suffering from long-term addiction to drugs has steadily grown.[2] In 1992 half of the women enrolling in treatment services had been using for five years or more. By 1998, 42 percent had been addicted for at least eleven years.[3]

Early intervention for drug-exposed children should begin not with their participation in infant and toddler educational programs. Rather, it should begin when drug-abusing women are pregnant and should be approached from education and public health perspectives. Pregnant drug-abusing women have been a major public health issue since the mid-1980s. Although considerable efforts and resources have been directed toward preventing drug use during pregnancy, many of these women continue to bear children who have been prenatally exposed. As a result, prenatal substance abuse, which was once considered only a public health problem, has become an issue that education professionals must begin to address. Although the impairment of drug-exposed children entering the public school systems are not as severe as suggested in early public health warnings, these children do have related conditions that can be mitigated through proper health care. As research has consistently pointed out, maternal health and the quality of prenatal care are two of the most important factors impacting the outcomes of children born to drug-abusing women. These children have fewer follow-up health care maintenance visits, are less likely to have completed immunizations, and spend more days in the hospital in comparison to other infants and toddlers.[4] Therefore, public health efforts should not only be directed toward preventing drug abuse during pregnancy. Rather, they must begin promote maternal health care for drug-abusing women as part of the intervention process for their children.

Education professionals must work in unison with public health officials to make maternal health for pregnant drug-abusing women a serious social and public health policy concern. Many new maternal and prenatal care and substance abuse programs were implemented to target this population during the late 1980s and early 1990s. However, more emphasis should be directed toward strengthening these programs. Many have suffered from a reduction in funding, which limits the number of women they are able to serve.[5] Other programs have shut down completely.[6] Since efforts to prevent drug-exposed births have not been successful and the associated disabilities are now an educational problem, the need for these specially focused maternal health programs is critical.

The need to encourage more drug-abusing women to utilize maternal and prenatal health and drug treatment services should also become a focus of public health policy. Many urban hospitals still offer prenatal health care to drug-abusing women; they have also implemented counseling services and regularly refer these families to other necessary resources.[7] However, not enough women fully embrace and participate in these programs. Many still turn away from such programs to avoid punitive attitudes and sanctions, and they often will not see a doctor until they are experiencing complications or it is time for delivery. As the trend toward punitive social welfare policies continues, we can expect more drug-abusing women needing these services to turn away from such programs, as this can jeopardize their eligibility for housing and public assistance. Therefore, public health efforts must expand beyond making these programs available and also work toward reversing the trend of punitive social policies; they must begin eliminating the barriers that keep drug-abusing women from using whatever early intervention services are available.

New focused efforts should make the case that implementing punitive policies and practices for pregnant drug-abusing women and mothers with young children is a public health problem, ultimately contributing to developmental disabilities. Some health care facilities have already started to address this problem from a public health perspective and discontinued the practice of reporting drug-abusing women to the authorities.[8] However, many facilities have adopted alternative punitive policies. Although not criminally oriented, such practices continue to deter drug-abusing expecting mothers from using prenatal and maternal health care services, as they risk losing custody of their children. It is important to draw more attention to the negative impacts of these practices on educational outcomes, as it is essential that the early intervention process begin during pregnancy. Early childhood practitioners, family-focused treatment centers, and health care professionals all must shed light on how these policies ultimately prevent children from receiving the help that they need.

National attention should not only focus on the developmental struggles of drug-affected children but also highlight their potential to reach appropriate developmental milestones. Better-informed public health messages would both highlight the lack of attention given to prenatal and maternal health care as part of the early intervention process and also clear up some of the public misconceptions about children born prenatally exposed to drugs. This is an important step, as two commonly held but mistaken assumptions have turned national attention away from the need to support these children's developmental issues. One such misconception is that crack or polydrug exposure totally destroys intellectual functioning and that attemps to help these children are a losing battle. The other, equally mistaken, is that children exposed to drugs in utero are almost free of any related developmental impairments and therefore it is not really necessary to give special attention to this issue. Correcting public misperceptions about drug-exposed children is especially important inasmuch as the sterilization campaign continues to reinforce the belief that drug-exposed babies are a biologically inferior population, thus supporting the idea that these children cannot be helped.

Drug-Exposed Babies and Part C of the Individuals with Disabilities Education Act

Programs that provide zero-to-three services under Part C of the IDEA should give more attention to the specific needs of the drug-affected population. Verification of drug exposure at birth should make these children automatically eligible for immediate early childhood interventions. Currently, infants who receive Part C services have serious birth-related problems or have spent time in a neonatal intensive care unit. These populations are particularly fragile and are understandably entitled to priority services. However, all states should be required to extend services to at-risk infants. This will allow drug-exposed babies to begin the intervention process at the start of life. Hospitals should coordinate with birth-to-three intervention programs to enroll these children immediately after birth. Many of the developmental challenges found in the school-age population are hard to detect at this stage. However, some subtle developmental impairments can be seen during infancy, indicating that they are at high risk for later early childhood delays and thus should be entitled to zero-to-three services.

Most importantly, birth-to-three programs should specifically target drug-exposed infants as part of their Child-Find recruitment agenda. These services aim to target infants at high risk for developmental delays, and the drug-exposed population is among the most needy. This entails developing better linkages with hospitals and other health care facilities to adequately identify drug-exposed newborns and their parents and enroll these families into the programs. Zero-to-three programs in communities where there are high concentrations of poverty and drug abuse should give particular attention to making these programs more accessible to drug-impacted families.

Addressing the needs of the drug-impacted population includes not only identifying children at birth, and enrolling them in early intervention programs, but also improving the type of services that they receive. One of the major issues seen with zero-to-three programs during the 1990s was that practitioners were never appropriately trained to work with the families of children with nontraditional disabilities, particularly those impacted by drug abuse.[9] The IDEA has acknowledged the need to train more highly qualified service providers for working with infants and toddlers with disabilities and their families.[10] Although some zero-to-three programs have since improved their services for at-risk infants and their families, these programs have a long way to go in terms of hiring an adequate number of highly qualified child development specialists.[11] In addition, they have not created a knowledge base for dealing specifically with drug-impacted infants and toddlers. It is extremely important that birth-to-three programs begin to give more attention to providing the appropriate developmental services to drug-impacted families with high-risk newborns. Intervention specialists working with this population will need to learn more about the related impairments and how to detect these problems at birth. Such programs should recommit to serving drug-impacted families, as "crack babies" were the major motivator behind the policy.

Throughout the 1990s, the results of studies regarding early childhood educators' experiences with drug-impacted children and their families demonstrated the need for more specific training. For example, a 1993 study reported that early childhood teachers had correct knowledge about birth outcomes and the health risks of pregnant drug-abusing women. However, they had no knowledge about how this condition affected the developmental progression of affected children or how to address these issues through early intervention services.[12] Another study published in 1995 surveyed eighty-five early childhood special educators (ECSEs) and eighty-eight Head Start educators (HSEs) regarding their preparation to work with drug-impacted preschoolers. Seventy-four percent of the ECSEs and 54 percent of the HSEs reported that they felt unprepared to work with these children.[13] In 1999 Kim, Sugai, and Kim surveyed early childhood educators about their experiences with drug-affected children. Similar to the aforementioned studies, the teachers reported having received little guidance in working with drug-affected children and believed that more training was needed to adequately serve this population.

Early intervention for drug-impacted families is a new area of early childhood educational studies. The need for these specialized services is growing, and the field needs to be further developed. Working with these families requires new skills, attitudes, and practices from service providers and calls for "a paradigm shift on the part of interventionist who [has] not dealt with issues of early childhood intervention as related to parental substance abuse."[14] Although traditional early intervention programs have embraced parenting education, the major focus has been directed toward child development. These conventional programs, while available to drug-affected children and their families and successful with other high-risk populations, are not as effective with families impacted by parental drug addiction.[15] Therefore, addressing the needs of both drug-impacted children and their parents should become the desired goal of early childhood professional development.

More effective family-focused programs should respond to drug-impacted families from a behavioral health perspective. In this context, early intervention services will begin to address all of the interrelated issues that affect parenting in drug-impacted families, ultimately improving the health and educational outcomes of children. These issues will include combining a variety of disciplines to provide substance abuse prevention and treatment, mental health services, and parenting intervention while also offering appropriate early childhood development interventions.

A step-by-step model is beyond the scope of this book. However, this work provides a rationale for adopting a behavioral health approach to early intervention with drug-impacted families. Bridging the gaps between the behavioral health services and early childhood education is easier talked about than done. Experts in both fields acknowledge the need to bring the two together but often disagree on how to achieve this goal. Addiction treatment professionals believe that after sobriety is achieved, a shift in identity will occur, and mothers will then be more successful in other areas such as parenting.[16] Child psychologists, on the other hand, make the argument that working on the parent-child relationship will encourage the identity shift necessary to achieve sobriety.[17]

To create useful, balanced, context-specific models, early intervention specialists must be committed to learning more about issues related to drug abuse and family systems. Interventionists must be trained to work with drug-abusing parents in a manner that best meets the parents' needs. They must evaluate their own attitudes toward crack/polydrug-abusing parents and examine how this may present obstacles to effectively working with these women. It is also important that early intervention providers gain professional knowledge about the nature of addictive behavior, particularly as it relates to child-rearing responsibilities, the relapsing nature of the disease, and the stigmas that have shaped societal attitudes about poor drug-abusing mothers and parenting.

Understanding the impact of addiction on the life experiences of drug-abusing mothers can also better prepare early intervention specialists to work with these women. Drug-abusing mothers have more intense parenting intervention needs.[18] The majority of these women have themselves had negative childhood experiences and suffer pathologies from childhood physical and sexual abuse and parental drug addiction.[19] These underlying issues may surface while addressing their own addiction problem and dealing with child rearing and development strategies. Therefore, it is necessary to have interventionists who are skilled in addressing the specific psychological needs of drug-abusing mothers.

Improving Preschool Interventions for Drug-Impacted Families: A Behavioral Health Approach

No matter how much effort is put into establishing access to health care for pregnant drug-abusing women and birth-to-three services for drug-exposed children, many children will not have the benefit of these early interventions. Therefore, their enrollment in preschool education programs is extremely important. Intervention at this stage is important for nonexposed children of drug-abusing parents as well. Unfortunately, there are complex issues involved with retaining families impacted by parental drug addiction after they enroll in early intervention programs. For a variety of reasons, children living in these situations are less likely to receive the full range of services, as these families are often not committed to participating in early intervention programs. Some may feel disenfranchised from the process because of prior negative experiences with early intervention providers.[20] Even when children are enrolled, maintaining contact with their parents can be difficult for service providers. Drug-abusing parents are difficult to track down; they move frequently, often miss appointments, many lack telephones, and even drop out of sight.[21] For these reasons, many drug-impacted children do not complete early intervention programs. These things affect the success rate of early interventions inasmuch as consistency is strongly correlated with successful outcomes.[22]

As with birth-to-three services, preschool programs should give more attention to recruiting the drug-impacted population. This high-risk population should be aggressively recruited for early intervention services. Emphasis should be placed on large-scale enrollment activities in communities where there is a high incidence of drug-exposed births. It is equally important that retention of these families become a specific focus of the early intervention agenda. Partnerships with human service agencies are necessary to help identify these families and to begin work toward addressing the preschool intervention issues with drug-exposed children. These collaborations are necessary to help eliminate the obstacles that prevent these families from fully participating in the programs.

Family-Focused Drug Treatment Programs and Early Intervention Services

Substance abuse programs focused on pregnant women and mothers with young children should become primary locations to implement early intervention services for drug-exposed children. These programs have broadened their scope to offer child care, prenatal and postnatal for both mother and child, housing, and other social services essential to the cohesiveness of drug-impacted families. Understandably, they have become the primary focus of comprehensive family-centered treatment models. However, such programs can do more to encourage drug-abusing mothers to pay more attention to the developmental outcomes of their children. Research has shown that although these women are often unable to balance their addiction with child-rearing responsibilities, they still feel obligated to their offspring.[23] This has been particularly evident with those who are in treatment. These mothers are more likely to embrace and consistently participate in early intervention programs than those who are not enrolled in treatment.

Unfortunately, most addiction treatment programs provide their clients very little information about how to cultivate the intellectual growth of their children.[24] Few offer interventions to children whose parents are participating in treatment services, and those that are available are for the most part inappropriate and ineffective.[25] Early childhood development interventions offered as part of some treatment programs have been known to place more emphasis on disciplinary issues rather than on educationally oriented exercises such as reading stories, developing social skills, and encouraging language development.[26]

Statistics on the developmental needs of drug-impacted children whose parents are in treatment demonstrate the need to combine early intervention with addiction treatment services.[27] Administrators in a residential drug treatment program in the Baltimore-Washington, D.C. area secured extra funding to examine the developmental needs of the children whose parents were in treatment.[28] The findings were alarming—the children's needs were far beyond what the program expected. Of all the children who had parents in treatment, 88 percent of the children tested positive for drug exposure. Fifteen percent qualified for services through the state of

Maryland's infant and toddler program due to the nature and degree of their developmental problems; 27 percent fell into the at-risk category for one or more of the developmental markers, placing them at high risk for developing more severe problems if not addressed early; and 23 percent had behavioral problems.[29] Such programs could better serve this population not only by addressing the developmental needs of children but also through working with early intervention programs to offer more developmentally appropriate models.

Integrating quality early intervention programs into treatment services targeting pregnant women and mothers with children has several benefits. First, empowering drug-abusing mothers to be responsible for their children is a powerful tool for recovery.[30] Some programs have found that when women become more involved in the lives of their children, they become more focused on treating their addiction.[31] This effect has been found to be particularly evident in those who are enrolled in treatment programs and have reached the recovery stage.[32] Second, drug-affected children will have the opportunity to participate in quality early intervention programs focused on the specific educational issues faced by drug impacted families. This will prepare these children for the school environment while also addressing the psychosocial risk factors of parental drug addiction. Most importantly, bridging these gaps will help stabilize these families, ultimately reducing the number of out-of-home placements.

Responding to the Needs of Schoolchildren: Recommendations for Programs, Practices, and Policies

Schools must put more effort into providing services for young children who are developmentally challenged but do not have permanent learning disabilities. Too many of these children are inappropriately placed in special education classes and labeled as having specific learning disabilities. As noted, this inappropriate labeling is a concern with young schoolchildren with developmental delays in general, but it is particularly a problem for the drug-impacted population. In an ideal situation, their issues should be addressed through educational services before they matriculate in school. The reality is that no matter how much effort is put into making sure that high-risk drug-exposed infants, toddlers, and preschoolers complete early intervention programs, many will not and so are extremely vulnerable to early school failure. In addition, while it is the goal of early intervention services to have children entering school functioning at an appropriate developmental level, these programs vary in terms of their effectiveness. Some provide good-quality services. But others have undertrained staff and are poorly run. Furthermore, these programs are still struggling to adequately address the needs of children impacted by drug exposure. As a result, some children who have already had early interventions will still require additional services when they enter school.

Although other early childhood school-based interventions are available, these programs have not been designed specifically for the needs of the drug-exposed population; as experts on educational interventions with drug-exposed school children have noted, "children with this history often do not respond to standard practices."[33] Therefore, while some of the more mildly affected children could possibly gain some benefits from such interventions, overall these services are inappropriate for the drug-exposed child. Therefore, it is necessary for public schools to work toward addressing the unique needs of the drug-exposed population. This process includes (1) identifying drug-exposed school children with developmental challenges, (2) designing educational assessments to detect their specific developmental problems, and (3) implementing effective classroom interventions and school-based support services to meet their needs.

Identifying Drug-Exposed Schoolchildren with Developmental Challenges

Early identification is extremely important to responding to the needs of drug-exposed schoolchildren with developmental challenges. Intervening as early as possible will help to prevent their mild delays or behavioral issues from developing into more serious problems. This process is particularly necessary for those who have not had the benefit of participating in preschool intervention programs. Public schools should not continue to let these children move through the system without ever receiving the appropriate interventions. Unfortunately, as teachers interviewed for this study have pointed out, schools currently have no systematic protocol for obtaining information regarding drug exposure status for the children who are enrolling. However, if public education is to begin seriously addressing the needs of these children, an organized system for gathering this information must be developed. Schools should begin to create linkages with hospitals, human service agencies, and other relevant community organizations to identify at-risk drug-exposed children for school-based intervention services.

Tracking systems are particularly needed in school communities where there is a high incidence of drug-exposed births. These communities must also work through the confidentiality and ethics issues, which often limit accessibility to background and medical information. It is important to identify drug-exposed schoolchildren with developmental challenges for two specific reasons. One, this will help protect these children from being mislabeled as having one of the traditional learning disabilities. The drug-exposed population will be recognized as youngsters demonstrating early childhood developmental delays but normal cognitive abilities. However, they are in need of interventions to correct these conditions. It is important that their developmental delays and behavioral problems be defined outside of the classifications used for children with traditional disabilities so that they are not inappropriately placed in early childhood special education classes. Two, if schools are going to begin seriously responding to the needs of drug-exposed children, they will need to provide the appropriate intervention, monitor the children's progress, and evaluate the effectiveness of school-based intervention programs.

Targeting Drug-Exposed Schoolchildren: A Double-Edged Sword

Identifying drug-exposed schoolchildren for educational purposes could have some unintended negative consequences. Information regarding drug exposure status should certainly be kept confidential and shared only with the necessary staff; however, having this information increases the likelihood that these children could be stigmatized in a way that will be harder to reverse as they move through the educational system, which presents a conflict to those who are concerned about addressing their educational difficulties. Nevertheless, if we continue to overlook the specific needs of drug-exposed children, we will contribute to their problems by letting their learning and behavioral issues be ignored.

Schools should commit to intervening on behalf of drug-exposed children with developmental challenges and make every effort possible to downplay any negative connotations associated with these children. These youngsters are more vulnerable to stigmatization than any other group of schoolchildren, as negative perceptions about prenatal crack/polydrug exposure outweigh the stigmas associated with children reared in poverty, students who are physically handicapped, and those who are labeled as special education students. Drug-exposed children have been constructed in the popular media as biologically inferior—a myth that researchers are still trying to erase. They have been used as the poster children for the war on drugs, which suggested that "crack kids" are the most severely neurologically damaged of all substance-exposed children. Despite new information regarding the cognitive development of drug-exposed children, many continue to believe this myth. Most damaging, however, is the targeting of their parents by a national sterilization campaign, further supporting the belief that these children are part of a biological underclass.

Teachers and other school personnel should avoid referring to drug-affected children as children as "crack babies," "crack kids," "drug babies," or any other negative term. They should dissuade other schoolchildren from using teose terms as well. Outside of receiving school-based interventions, these children should be treated no differently than their nonaffected peers. Public schools must make every effort to eliminate the negative terminology and stereotypes often attached to these children.

Toward School-Based Educational Assessments

As one Chicago public school teacher said,

> It's a waste of time trying to figure out what's wrong with a student and trying to provide them with the correct kinds of services if we don't know what we [are] looking for.

Learning which children have been exposed is an essential part of the public school intervention process. However, schools should not consider all drug-exposed children as high-risk solely on the basis of their birth history. Some drug-exposed children will have outgrown their developmental challenges and enter school at an appropriate developmental stage, ready to learn. Others, although exposed to drugs in utero, may never demonstrate developmental impairments. As pointed out in the medical review, variables such as the amount of drug used during pregnancy, the potency of the drug, maternal health and nutrition during pregnancy, the quality of prenatal care, and the caregiving environment all influence how drug exposure will impact developmental outcomes. There is no typical description of the drug-exposed child; their behaviors and learning problems vary, and not all are affected to the same degree. Therefore, schools will have to identify only those children needing support. To make this distinction, all drug-exposed children should be required to have an educational assessment when they enroll in school. Such evaluations should be given in addition to any other routine school assessments, even if the child has already participated in a preschool program.

It is also important that early childhood professionals develop and utilize school-based educational evaluations designed specifically for children impacted by drug exposure. The teachers interviewed in this study have acknowledged that the symptoms of drug exposure are often misinterpreted in young schoolchildren. Therefore, assessments must be made specifically for this population. Evaluations must be multifocal and comprehensive, designed to address all the issues that contribute to school failure in drug-impacted children. What happens between the time they are born and when they enter school plays a key role in their school readiness. Some will come from stable home environments. However, many drug-impacted school children are products of the foster care system or are living with their biological drug-abusing parents in high-risk environments, contributing to their developmental adversities. The intervention needs of each child will vary accordingly.

Standardized IQ test evaluations are not sufficient to determine the educational needs of drug-exposed schoolchildren.[34] These students' problems are often difficult to detect, and conventional early childhood assessments may fail to distinguish the characteristic symptoms.[35] As a consequence, many children needing intervention could be overlooked for services. More appropriate measurements are needed to detect their more subtle behavioral and learning problems, such as attention deficit, hyperactivity, information processing issues, and other self-control issues, which are likely to become more noticeable as children spend more time in school. Learning how to better detect these problems will allow these children to receive interventions before these issues develop into more serious disabilities. For example, one study asked first-grade teachers to evaluate the behavior problems found in a group of elementary school students, using two different types of assessments. One was a commonly used teacher rating scale; the other was an investigator-developed scale that was designed to identify the problems associated with prenatal drug exposure. Blind to the exposure status of the children, teachers scored the exposed children higher on the context-designed scale. However, these same children showed no differences on the general teacher rating scale.[36] Instruments designed to pinpoint the behavioral and learning difficulties associated with drug exposure will be valuable in determining the educational needs of each child.

Drug-impacted schoolchildren will most likely fall into one of three categories:

1. Children who have outgrown their developmental difficulties
2. Those who have milder impairments, such as short attention spans, mild hyperactivity, delayed speech and language development, and inconsistent learning patterns
3. Those who are more severely impacted, with major speech and language impairments, more intense emotional issues, and highly disruptive behavior or violent tendencies

After these evaluations are complete, schools will then be able to determine which intervention is most appropriate. Schools should make every effort to keep drug-exposed children in regular education classrooms. Thus far, special education programs themselves have not given enough attention to learning about the developmental challenges of drug-impacted school children and so have not adequately served this population. For this reason, although most of these children will have learning and behavioral problems, early childhood special education should be the last resort.

One of the major findings of this study is that although teachers expressed a willingness to give attention to the needs of drug-exposed children, they are disappointed about the lack of guidance in working with these students, particularly those who have demonstrated the potential for normal achievement. This concern was one of the major focuses of the interviews and drew attention to the fact that public schools really have not provided classroom teachers with the information and resources they need. Although some information is available on working specifically with school-age drug-affective children, this knowledge has not been widely disseminated in urban public school systems. In order to better accommodate these students, schools must commit to learning more about how to respond to the needs of the drug-affected population and training teachers to work with these children in regular classrooms.

Educating Drug-Impacted Schoolchildren: Best Practices or Responsive Classroom Model

Since prenatal drug exposure affects children differently, schools should consider adopting two classroom interventions—a best-practices approach for regular education classrooms and a Responsive Classroom Model for the more severely impacted children who also have emotional problems.

Dr. Ira Chasnoff and colleagues studied effective intervention with drug-exposed schoolchildren and, like the public school teachers interviewed for this study, concluded that these youngsters require "more direct and aggressive classroom interventions than children with behavioral problems that are not prenatally exposed."[37] This research, published as *Understanding the Drug-Exposed Child: Approaches to Behavior and Learning* offers a best-practices guide to working with drug-exposed schoolchildren. This text offers approaches to managing drug-exposed children in regular education classes, focusing particularly on the challenging behavioral problems. This is an excellent start for teachers who desire to learn more about research-based classroom interventions for school-age children. The strategies offered could benefit more mildly impaired children, who would be classified as part of the second group. These children have great potential but will need to be supported as they move through the educational system. With developmentally appropriate classroom practices, these youngsters are more likely to successfully meet the challenges of a general education setting.

Understanding the Drug-Exposed Child is divided into three sections: the research basis of intervention strategies, principles of child behavior and classroom management, and guidelines for the development of individual behavior interventions. The classroom interventions are excellent and will help to prevent these youngsters from being removed from regular education settings. Though based on research, these strategies are remarkably similar to those gathered from the veteran public-school teachers who participated in the present study. However, school administrators have the ultimate responsibility to support teachers in learning more about how they can successfully accommodate these children in regular education settings and providing the extra needed classroom assistance.

Children in the third group will need a more intensive intervention strategy. Their aggressive behavior, emotional issues, and severe self-regulatory problems make these children more difficult to handle in a regular classroom setting, and a regular general education class may not be the best starting point, as it may set them up for later school failure. Nonetheless, schools should still consider working with these children outside the realm of special education.

One option is to work with these youngsters in specially designed full-inclusion settings. Here children benefit from best practices and also receive additional early childhood developmental services within the full-inclusion setting. Specially designed full-inclusion classrooms should have a low student-to-teacher ratio, allowing each child to receive the individual attention needed to improve in his or her weak areas. Teachers should be provided with full-time classroom assistance from professionals who are trained in specific problem areas. Such settings will allow children to receive more individual, specialized attention and remain outside special education classrooms. This will also allow drug-exposed children to cultivate their intellectual abilities and develop appropriate social skills before they are presented with the challenges of a regular general education atmosphere.

Schools interested in working with more severely impacted drug-affected children outside the circle of special education may consider adopting the responsive classroom model used in Project DAISY, the program that was implemented in four Washington, D.C., public schools during the early 1990s. As is the case with the best practices offered by Chasnoff and associates, the developer of the responsive classroom model points out that these strategies are also appropriate for nonexposed schoolchildren who are from stressful environments and who have developmental challenges.

Two aspects of the Project DAISY model will be useful in guiding school-based interventions. First, children in the program received three years of consistent intervention services and remained with the same teacher throughout this period; preschool children enrolled in the project at an average of 2.9 years of age and remained in the program until they reached school age. Some had more noticeable behavioral problems combined with other psychosocial issues. Each class had no more than fifteen children. The typical setup included seven exposed children and seven nonexposed children. The exposed children had a documented history of prenatal drug exposure and related developmental impairments, which supports the argument for proper identification and evaluation.

The aspect of the program that was potentially most useful was that children received intensive specialized early childhood development services within their classroom, eliminating the need for outside special education services. The responsive classroom model incorporated early childhood professionals and developmental specialists; their purpose was to assist the project leader and target specific problem areas. The intervention team included a trained project teacher and educational assistant, two skilled speech and language pathologists and two interns training in the field, two clinical psychologists, a movement specialist, a nutritionist, and a social worker. Each specialist played an important part in organizing classroom activities to better accommodate these children in a highly structured full-inclusion setting.

Dr. Diane Powell, former director of Project DAISY and current director of the Student Intervention Services Branch for the Washington, D.C., public schools, discussed the rationale behind integrating drug-exposed children with special needs into classroom settings with their nonexposed peers. As she put it, "children learn how to act and behave by modeling others."[38] She feels that "teaching these children in isolation is not a good strategy," even if they require extra services.[39] Therefore, the pullout services offered in some public school full-inclusion settings, although designed for children with developmental delays, would not benefit the drug-impacted population. In an article explaining developmentally appropriate educational interventions for substance-exposed children, Powell explained:

> It is necessary for teachers to understand the developmental needs of their students and organize the classroom environment to support those needs.... [W]hen children need related service support such as speech-language intervention and play therapy, those services should be integrated into the child's activities within the classroom.[40]

Approximately 120 schoolchildren in the Washington, D.C., area participated in Project DAISY. After completing the program, these children transitioned into regular education classrooms at the same schools where they received the interventions.[41] Information about drug-exposure status was kept confidential and available only to the project staff; teachers in regular education classes had no information on which children were exposed.

The responsive classroom model could be used as a school-based alternative to special education for drug-affected children. These children could be placed in a responsive classroom until the third grade. After this period, these children will be better prepared to function in a regular education classroom with a larger number of students and fewer adult interventions, giving them a better chance at academic success.

Social Work Services in the Schools and Drug-Impacted Children

School-based interventions for drug-affected children should not be limited only to those who were prenatally exposed. Rather, they should include resources for nonexposed students of drug-abusing parents. This group of drug-impacted youngsters cannot be identified for early childhood intervention by substance exposure status. As discussed, parental drug addiction has placed many children at equal risk for school failure, and they will also need school-based support services. The fragmented and limited services currently offered in many public schools are lacking the knowledge and resources needed to work with this population.

These youngsters have diverse home situations, which could include living with biological parents, foster parents, grandparents or other relatives, or even in homeless shelters. Caregivers are often not provided with adequate resources to assist them with caring for these children. This is particularly an issue with many grandparents and other relatives who are raising children born to drug-abusing parents. They are not always provided with the same level of support as foster parents are, and as the children grow older child welfare services become less involved in working with these families. It would benefit drug-impacted children if school professionals would become more involved in attending to their health and human service needs.

Although these services will be coordinated at the school, home visits should become a part of the school intervention plan. Full-time professionals who are trained as specialists in working with families impacted by substance abuse should provide such services. Similar to early intervention programs, developing awareness about poor families impacted by drug abuse is a virtual prerequisite for the school practitioners to work with these families. Such issues will become more important as the social problems with schoolchildren become more of an issue. Support staff should have background knowledge regarding all the issues underlying parental drug addiction within low-income communities. They should learn about the stigmas placed upon these families and the myths and realities about poor urban drug-abusing women and their children. They must also have knowledge of current social polices affecting drug-impacted families and the impact that they have on young schoolchildren.

Public schools should also coordinate the interagency collaborations necessary to adequately support the diversity of needs within drug-impacted families. Such partnerships will help to provide the full range of services needed to cultivate the healthy growth and academic development of drug-impacted children. They will also allow schools to benefit from community resources, improving the quality of school-based social support systems.

It is important that schools be prepared to address the mental health issues found in children of drug-abusing parents. This is important for both exposed and nonexposed children. As previously pointed out, these children suffer from emotional imbalances resulting from insecure attachments and other traumatic experiences while living with their biological parents and while in the foster care system. The Substance Abuse and Mental Health Services evaluation of mental health services for children from drug-impacted families demonstrates the necessity for giving attention to mental health issues. The evaluation documented that over 60 percent of the children in treatment for emotional disturbances come from families with substance abuse problems.[42] Children from substance abuse situations also encountered family violence, sexual abuse, and physical abuse, circumstances that adversely affected their emotional well-being.[43] This study supports the belief that without proper intervention, the problems escalate as they grow older and move through the educational system. The older children had more psychiatric hospitalizations, attempted suicide more often, and had histories of running away from home.[44] These statistics highlight the need for schools to more effectively intervene by offering multifocal clinical interventions to address these complex issues.

Educationally Focused Support Groups for Caregivers

The caregivers of drug-impacted children will benefit from support groups organized by public schools. These groups can encourage parents to become more active in the educational development of drug-affected children and to come together around the developmental challenges of children impacted by prenatal drug exposure. It would be most helpful if classroom teachers working with these children and other involved school practitioners facilitated these support groups. This will also allow parents to become more familiar with the school, the educational needs of these children, and effective at-home strategies, and to learn more about school-based support services.

One particular benefit is that support groups can motivate caregivers to organize on behalf of drug-affected youngsters. Currently, with the exception of the National Association for Families and Addiction Research and Education (NAFARE), there are no organizations consistently advocating on behalf of improving the educational outcomes of drug-exposed schoolchildren. Although the crack baby crisis is no longer a media sensation, prenatal drug exposure is still a problem, and affected children continue to enroll in school. Parents of other children with special needs have protested to ensure that their children's problems are addressed within the public education arena, which is committed to a "free and appropriate" education for all students. Their efforts have led to education programs and services that address the specific developmental challenges of their children. The caregivers of drug-affected children can also mobilize on behalf of these high-risk students. The parents know firsthand the difficulties that these children are facing and can be powerful allies in the fight for their educational programs and policies.

Supporting Educational Interventions for Schoolchildren

Obtaining funding for programs for school-age drug-impacted children would probably be more successful at the local level. Improving social work services in schools will require the appropriate financial support to attract the needed full-time professionals. Likewise, schools that want to help these children outside of special education classes will have to make the case for specially designed, family-focused, school-based interventions, particularly those that would use the responsive classroom model. Since the 1980s the movement toward full-service schools—educational services that support the needs of the community—has grown. School-based family support services have relied on a variety of funding sources, such as the Comprehensive School Reform Demonstration (CSRD) program, the 21st Century Community Learning Centers, and the Community for Learning program.[45] These federally funded programs are typically used to support schoolwide comprehensive programs focusing on improving classroom teaching, ultimately improving student achievement, and could be used to support educational interventions for drug-impacted schoolchildren. There was also increased understanding among educators during the 1990s that "if the non-educational needs that poor children bring to the classroom go un-addressed, the children will not succeed at school no matter how effective the instruction."[46] At the same time, it is understood that "schools alone cannot be expected to educate youngsters with severe health and social problems that inhibit their ability to learn, supporting the need for better social work services in the schools."[47] This perspective helped to support funding for social service reforms in schools, particularly in districts with large numbers of high-risk young children.

Although the school-reform funding sources mentioned embrace the concept of school-community linkages, it may still be difficult to justify services specifically for drug-affected children under these programs, as this is still a controversial issue and these programs historically have funded whole-school reform efforts. However, professional development of teachers and improvement of student outcomes are a focus of these programs. Schools could still advocate for educational services for drug-impacted children through these programs. Drug-affected children will need instructional models to accommodate their particular learning styles. Also, working with the biological parents or caregivers of drug-affected children requires different approaches. Collaborative services in the context of school reform could be extended to other needy students and are an option worth considering.

Schools could also consider applying for categorical grants to support programs for drug-affected children. Categorical funding is used to support educational services with a specific objective that is not covered by other funding sources. These grants also give school districts and local schools more control in addressing their specific needs. The opportunities for funding vary from state to state, but this is another excellent resource for funding developmentally appropriate school-based programs for drug-exposed children and their families.

Governmental support for school-based drug prevention and intervention programs should be extended to support the educational needs of drug-impacted children. Thus far these children have not been able to claim a share of the funding allocated to support public school responses to the urban drug problem. School districts should also consider tapping into these resources. They would be appropriate to support school-based social services for the drug-impacted population, as they are concerned with the education of disadvantaged children.[48]

Drug-Exposed Schoolchildren as an Educational Policy Issue

The educational policy question regarding drug-exposed schoolchildren has been and remains a complex issue. However, if schools are going to begin responding to the educational dilemmas posed by this population, this issue must be revisited. To some degree, these children should become an educational policy issue. This book has shown that most educational professionals agree many of the problems detected in school-age drug-exposed children can be addressed without the need for special education placement. Public education must become committed to learning more about how to accommodate these children in general education classes, provide professional development for teachers, and develop better school-based social support services. However, urban public schools already struggle to provide intervention services for at-risk children in general. And although drug-impacted children need more specialized intervention strategies, school-based programs for young children with developmental delays are already offered. Classroom strategies for working specifically with drug-exposed children with developmental challenges are suggested in this text. However, public schools may not put sufficient effort into identifying and working with these children outside special education programs.

Therefore, although incorporating intervention strategies into regular education classes is advocated and special education placement is the less desirable option, this may continue to be the only alternative, as school-district-initiated programs for drug-impacted children vanished during the 1990s. Prenatal drug exposure results in developmental challenges that impact educational experiences. Responding to children with birth-related impairments is a direct responsibility of special education services. Therefore, it is important that we begin to explore how the Individuals with Disabilities Education Act (IDEA) can be used as a vehicle for addressing the needs of drug-exposed school children.

The amendments made to the IDEA during the 1990s acknowledged children outside the traditional disability categories who also need special educational interventions. This demonstrates the intention of the IDEA to respond to all children with educational challenges. However, every effort must be made to ensure that drug-exposed children are made eligible for services under this legislation. This option should be available even if schools chose to work with these children in general education settings, for professional development for teachers and school-based social services will need to be supported. Every effort should be made to classify these children under the new developmental delay category, which has been extended to schoolchildren who need intervention but who do not fit into any of the traditional classifications.

Eligibility requirements for the developmental delay category are largely determined by the states, which will have to be more definitive in including drug-exposed children. Although each state has its own formula for deciding which children will be served, two specific things will have to be done in response to school-age drug-exposed children. One, all states should make drug-impacted children eligible to be served under this category. As explained, this is important to ensure that drug-exposed children who do not have serious mental or physical conditions and nonexposed children of drug-abusing parents are also identified as at-risk and are therefore made eligible for services. Defining drug-exposed children under the developmental delay classification will also help take away some of the special education stigma inasmuch as this category is for children who are developmentally delayed but not mentally retarded or severely handicapped. These children could be classified as students who have normal cognitive capabilities but who have developmental challenges resulting from drug exposure and therefore need the services.

Two, to strengthen the commitment to a "free and appropriate education" for all children with special needs, the IDEA must not only acknowledge the drug-affected population but also guarantee them developmentally appropriate interventions. Special education must become more committed to helping young children with nontraditional developmental delays reach their full potential and be successful in general education classrooms. What is offered in special education is insufficient for meeting the needs of developmentally delayed students in general.[49] Such programs continue to be limited in the quality of services they can provide to students, as these programs suffer from teacher shortages and a lack of high-qualified personnel.[50] Current practices used in these setting will be even more inappropriate for drug-affected children.

The 1997 IDEA amendments focused on improving teaching and learning by addressing the disabilities that affect "child involvement and progress" in a general education curriculum.[51] However, the law does not specifically mandate that teachers incorporate best practices to help children be successful in a general education setting, which is extremely important for drug-exposed children with behavioral issues. The legislation requires that teachers document "measurable progress" but does not stipulate that such improvement must result in grade-level functioning. "Measurable progress" could be interpreted in many ways, which often does not help children in the long term or prepare them to successfully meet the challenges of a general education classroom. As a result, although many children with correctable disabilities receive special education services, it is nearly impossible for them to be successful in regular education settings. Therefore, if services are supported under the auspices of special education, they must be designed according to the responsive classroom model or the best-practices interventions provided by Chasnoff and associates.

Acknowledging drug-exposed children under special education policy is also important for those who may not benefit from general education placement at all. After almost two decades of conflicting, methodologically flawed studies, research is just beginning to make a direct connection between drug exposure and possible long-term developmental impairment.[52] Research in this area still has a long way to go. Although it is hoped that preschool or school-based interventions will help some children, others will need an alternative educational placement. Thus, should also be supported under the IDEA.

Expanding the Knowledge Base
Building the educational knowledge base on drug-effected children is of the utmost importance. This is the only way to develop effective educational policy and programs. Education professionals must become more proactive in contributing to the literature on how drug exposure impacts schoolchildren and what are effective intervention practices. Other populations with birth-related developmental challenges have been clearly defined and appropriately studied, and the drug-impacted population de-

serves their space. Some of the developmental difficulties identified by public-school teachers, such as speech and language delays and ADD/ADHD, are similar to the problems detected in preschoolers and are shared by other schoolchildren with developmental delays. Although these issues may be more severe with drug-exposed children, schools have some knowledge regarding intervention strategies. However, some of the behavioral and learning pratterns particular to the drug-exposed population are not common early childhood issues and warrant further investigation.

For example, more research into the inconsistent learning patterns detected in schoolchildren is particularly needed. As discussed, this results in children being inappropriately labeled as learning-disabled and subsequently placed in early childhood special education. Attention should also be given to the unusual emotional temperament displayed by some drug exposed school children. As with other behavioral issues such as ADD and ADHD, this presents barriers to keeping these children in regular education settings. According to veteran schoolteachers, children with the aforementioned developmental challenges can at times learn as well as other students. This raises questions about how schools define behavioral and learning problems in young children and supports the need to develop a better understanding of children with nontraditional learning disabilities.

Professional Development of Teachers

Early childhood and special education teacher preparation programs must begin to give more attention to preparing teachers to cope with children who do not respond to traditional instruction but do not necessarily need out-of-classroom placement. This should be a specific priority for programs that are preparing educational professionals to work in urban school districts. These programs should make a concerted effort to train teachers to respond to learner diversity issues. Such programs should study the school-age drug-exposed child independently from other special needs children. Their educational dilemmas are much different from those of other high-risk children in that most of their issues are just beginning to be understood.

Most importantly, if schools do become committed to improving the educational outcomes of drug-exposed children and serving these children outside the circle of special education, teachers who are currently working in classrooms must be provided with the opportunity to gain further understanding of how to address the particular needs of these students. Experience has given veteran teachers more knowledge about classroom interventions with these children. However, many teachers who have an interest in the development of drug-exposed children find it difficult to respond to their educational needs, as they lack an understanding of effective intervention practices. Both teachers and students will benefit from in-services about children with unconventional developmental challenges who remain in general education settings. This is a concern not only with the drug-exposed population but also with young children with correctible early childhood developmental delays in general.

Evaluating School-Based Interventions

Programs and classroom practices used with the school-age population must be evaluated as to their effects on student outcomes. This will allow schools to offer the most effective interventions possible to drug-exposed children. Most importantly, it will contribute to the knowledge base on children with nontraditional developmental issues by not only paying attention to the nature of the disability but also offering research-based information on the effectiveness of intervention programs and practices. The best-practices and responsive classroom models offered in this book are an excellent starting point for schools. However, they are only the beginning. One of the limitations of the early intervention demonstration projects developed by various school districts during the late 1980s and early 1990s is their lack of longitudinal follow-up on the participating children. These programs were successful in recruiting drug-exposed children with developmental delays and providing the early interventions deemed necessary to prepare these children for school. However, little is known about what happened to this specific group of students as they grew older and moved through the public school system. Even less is known about the long-term effectiveness of the district-initiated family-centered interventions for drug-impacted families with preschoolers.

Early childhood education research must begin to produce more definitive information on the effectiveness of specialized early intervention with drug-exposed children. This is particularly important for models that are to be used in family-focused drug-treatment programs. Research will have to examine the effectiveness of combining disciplines to best target drug-abusing women in treatment and their children. Studies will need to provide the information needed to strengthen such intervention programs to achieve the maximum benefit to both parent and child. This information will be particularly useful when the benefits of specialized programs are examined in comparison to early intervention models commonly offered in drug-treatment programs. This will also help support the need for more education-related social policies focusing specifically on the drug-exposed population.

What Does This Study Tell Us about School Reform, Educational Policy, and At-Risk Children?

Educational interventions for at-risk students must begin to address all the factors that contribute to early school failure. Many school reform intervention programs are primarily focused on improving teacher instructional practices and changing school culture. These things are essential to strengthening the quality of education offered in public schools. Thus, improving learner outcomes. However, this is only one aspect of a multi-dimensional problem. There are many barriers that contribute to the poor academic achievement of children in traditionally low performing districts. In the process of reforming public schools, initiatives must become stronger in strengthening three important areas: (1) the instructional needs of the diverse learner; (2) school-based family support services; and (3) comprehensive health care and social services.

Learner Diversity: School reform programs giving particular attention to instructional practices must begin to address learner diversity needs. Not all students respond to one instructional practice. Classroom teachers must be prepared to teach all children (those without traditional disabilities) regardless of their learning styles. These programs must also be able to reach those children with non-traditional learning challenges. These programs must design curriculums and incorporate strategies to help these children reach appropriate developmental milestones and remain within a regular education setting. The diverse learner is in almost every classroom and many low-performing urban districts will need to learn how to respond to the instructional needs of these students. Urban school reform models and teacher preparation programs cannot be totally successful without addressing this issue.

Focus on Parental Support: School reform programs have given more attention to parental involvement since the 1980s. However, schools have not done a good job of reaching out to families and engaging them in the educational experiences of their children. School initiated family support programs must begin to do a better job of working with parents, as the homeschool-relationship is a critical aspect of improving student outcomes, and ultimately improving schools. Such programs result in stronger parent and teacher relationships, develop a respect for the educational services provided by the school, and help to create a culture of learning among the school, family, and the community. Implementing family support programs is challenging, particularly in communities with long-standing social problems that impact family functioning, and ultimately student learning. However, schools that are serious about working with these families must be committed to addressing these issues and work through the barriers that prevent these programs from being successful.

Full-Scale Health and Social Services: This is a very important, but often overlooked aspect of addressing early school failure. This is not only in the context of neglected children from drug-impacted backgrounds, but youngsters from high-risk environments in particular. Even if the best practices and family support were offered, children will need to have their health care, immunizations, nutrition and other related needs met to be ready to learn. Educational professionals can no longer take the position that this is not school responsibility. To reform schools to meet the needs of the most vulnerable students in the most troubled districts, policymakers must begin to include health and social services as a major component of school reform initiatives.

Addressing these specific areas of school intervention programs will not only improve the school community as a whole, but will also make children more receptive to the learning atmosphere. Thus, resulting in better overall district outcomes.

Summary and Conclusions

There is no simple way to address the complex developmental needs of children impacted by drug exposure; this book is only the beginning of the discussion. It continues to be a struggle to get educational policies and programs designed to meet their specific needs, as this population has not yet secured a space on the policy agenda. The lack of attention given to their developmental challenges has made the academic failure of these children a self-fulfilling prophecy. Although they could surmount many of their educational barriers, drug-affected children are not given the chance to develop their potential in the current system. Their developmental difficulties have been alternately both exaggerated and oversimplified. On some level, these youngsters really are no different from their peers reared in poverty. They are enrolled in schools in neighborhoods where there are high concentrations of poverty, academic achievement is low, programs are underfunded, per-pupil expenditures are low, and there are teacher shortages. Most disappointing is that special education program are understaffed, are filled with untrained professionals, and offer no real solutions for students who, with developmentally appropriate interventions, could return to general education classes and thrive in those settings. Therefore, as is true of many of their nonexposed peers, they are destined to special education placement, which has not been very effective in schools located in poor communities.

Since the late 1980s, parental drug addiction in poor families has spurred many disciplines to acknowledge this population's needs and design interventions accordingly. Addiction treatment programs altered their modalities to respond to the needs of pregnant women and mothers with children. Human services have also adopted new intervention models to address the myriad issues of families impacted by parental drug addiction. Educational professionals must also become more involved in addressing the needs of drug-affected children. It is important that their developmental needs are appropriately addressed at the preschool, public school, and educational policy levels. If this happens, we will hear less about how drug-affected children are falling through the cracks and more about their educational resiliency.

APPENDIX A
Data Collection Instrument

Questionnaire

Section 1: Demographic Information

1. Location of employment: 1. Chicago _____
                             2. Champaign_____
                             3. Baltimore _____

2. Gender: 1 _____ Male   2 _____ Female

3. Race: 1 _____ Black
             2 _____ White
             3 _____ Other

4. Age range of children you work with:_____

5. Years of teaching experience: _____

6. Years of experience with drug-exposed children _____

7. Years of experience with special-needs children_____

8. Do you feel you can adequately identify drug-exposed children?

   1. Yes _____
   2. No _____

How would you describe the drug-exposed child?

How do you know when a child is exposed to drugs?

1. Word of mouth _____

2. School records_____

3. Some other source _____(specify)

Section II: Behavior and Learning Problems

This section is designed to learn more about the developmental challenges of school-age drug-exposed children and to determine if the behavioral and learning problems detected in preschoolers are prevalent within the school population. Using the Likert scale, please respond to the following statements:

1 = Strongly Agree, 2 = Agree, 3 = Neither Agree or Disagree,
4 = Disagree, 5 = Strongly Disagree

9. Children born prenatally exposed to drugs have delays in speech and language skill.   1 2 3 4 5

10. Children born prenatally exposed to drugs have problems with processing information.   1 2 3 4 5

11. Children born prenatally exposed to drugs lose control easily.   1 2 3 4 5

12. Children born prenatally exposed to drugs are easily distracted.   1 2 3 4 5

13. Children prenatally exposed to drugs have difficulty staying on task.   1 2 3 4 5

14. Children born prenatally exposed to drugs have mood swings.   1 2 3 4 5

15. Children born prenatally exposed to drugs have problems moving from one task to another.   1 2 3 4 5

Please indicate any learning or behavior problems that you find are common in drug-exposed children that have not been mentioned.

What things do you find to be most problematic with drug-exposed children in the classroom?

Section III: Teaching Drug-Exposed Children

16. Children born prenatally exposed to drugs/crack   1 2 3 4 5
    exhibit learning and behavioral problems that
    are different from other special-needs children.

17. Children born prenatally exposed to drugs require   1 2 3 4 5
    different teaching and behavioral strategies than
    other children.

18. My teacher education preparation provided me   1 2 3 4 5
    with the knowledge I need to work with
    drug-exposed children.

19. Teacher education programs should incorporate   1 2 3 4 5
    courses to adequately prepare teachers to work
    with drug-exposed children in the classroom.

20. Teachers should be able to identify drug-exposed   1 2 3 4 5
    children and distinguish their problems from
    other special-needs populations.

21. Drug-exposed children should be kept in   1 2 3 4 5
    mainstream classrooms.

22. I personally would like more training about   1 2 3 4 5
    the special needs of drug exposed children.

What teaching strategies do you find to be effective with drug-exposed children?

Section IV: Media Perceptions and Research Knowledge
Can you recall any news stories or documentaries about drug-exposed children? If so, please tell me about them.

Please respond to the follow statements using the same scale.

23. Most crack-exposed children test within the   1 2 3 4 5
    normal range cognitively.

24. Most children born exposed to crack are   1 2 3 4 5
    severely neurologically damaged.

25. Most crack-exposed children will never achieve   1 2 3 4 5
    appropriate social, emotional, and educational
    levels.

APPENDIX B
Demographic Information

Profile of Teachers

City	Gender	Race	Grade level	Years teaching	Years with D/E children	Years with S/N children	Ability to identify D/E children
1	2	3	2	8	8	2	1
1	2	2	1	8	5	2	1
1	2	2	3	22	12	16	3
1	2	1	4/5	30	10	20	3
1	2	1	1	20	10	0	3
1	2	1	0	28	10	5	1
2	2	1	6	30	10	9	3
2	2	1	7	25	12	20	3
2	2	1	6	23	10	20	3
2	2	1	1	21	10	15	1
2	2	1	7	25	10	0	3
3	2	1	7	25	15	0	3
3	2	1	1	31	15	0	3
3	1	1	3	6	6	0	1
3	2	1	7	10	10	0	1
3	2	1	3	22	10	0	3

D/E = Drug-exposed

S/N = Special-needs

City: 1 = Champaign   Gender: 1 = Male   Race: 1 = Black
        2 = Cook County   2 = Female   2 = White
        3 = Baltimore   3 = Other

Grade level/age range: 0 = Kindergarten   Ability to identify D/E children: 1 = Yes
                           1 = First grade   2 = No
                           2 = Second grade   3 = Sometimes
                           3 = Third grade
                           4 = Fourth grade
                           5 = Fifth grade
                           6 = K-5 specialist
                           7 = Middle school

APPENDIX C
Survey/Questionnaire Results

Behavioral and Learning Problems

	Strongly Agree	Agree	Neither Agree/nor Disagree	Strongly Disagree	Disagree	Total
Speech and language	9	3	4	0	0	16
Processing information	10	5	1	0	0	16
Easily distracted	16	0	0	0	0	16
Lose control	14	2	0	0	0	16
Staying on task	16	0	0	0	0	16
Mood swings	11	4	1	0	0	16
Changing task	11	5	0	0	0	16

Teaching Drug-Exposed Children

	Strongly Agree	Agree	Neither Agree/nor Disagree	Strongly Disagree	Disagree	Total
Different from other special needs students	4	8	3	1	0	16
Different teaching and behavioral strategies	11	4	1	0	0	16
Teacher preparation provided proper knowledge	4	1	0	2	9	16
Should be able to distinguish drug-exposed children	6	3	3	3	1	16
Would like more training	8	7	1	0	0	16

Media Perceptions/Research Knowledge

	Strongly Agree	Agree	Neither Agree/nor Disagree	Strongly Disagree	Disagree	Total
Test within the normal range	2	2	8	3	1	16
Severely neurologically damaged	1	4	10	0	1	16
Will never achieve appropriate levels	0	2	12	2	0	16

Notes

Foreword

1. Taylor, S., Rizvi, F., Lindgard, B., and Henry, M., *Educational policy and the politics of change* (London: Routledge, 1997).
2. Young, M. D., Multifocal educational policy research. Toward a method for enhancing traditional policy studies, *American Educational Research Journal*, 36 (1999), 677–714; Scheurich, J. J., Policy archeology: A new policy studies mythology, *Journal of Education Policy*, 9 (1994), 297–316; Ball, S., *Education reform: A critical and poststructural approach* (Buckingham, England: Open University Press, 1994. Dunbar, C. (2001). *Does anyone know were here: Alternative schooling for African American youth*. New York: Peter Lang. Pillow, W. S. (1997). Decentering silences/troubling irony: Teen pregnancy's challenge to policy analysis. In C. Marshall (Ed.), *Feminist critical policy analysis: A perspective from primary and secondary schooling* (pp. 134–152). London: Falmer Press.

Introduction

1. Kusserow, R. P., *Crack babies,* Report of the Office of the Inspector General (Washington, D.C.: Department of Health and Human Services, 1990).
2. Ibid.

Chapter 1

1. Fraser, N., *Unruly practices: Power discourse and gender in contemporary social theory.* Minneapolis: University of Minnesota Press.
2. Reeves, J. L., and Campbell, R., *Crack coverage: Television, news, the anti-drug crusade and the Reagan legacy* (Durham: Duke University Press, 1994).
3. Reeves and Campbell, *Crack coverage.*
4. Ibid., 208.
5. Ibid.
6. Ibid. This issue is discussed in more detail in Reinarman, C., and Levine, H. G., *Crack in America: Demon drugs and social justice* (Berkeley: University of California Press, 1997).
7. Ibid.
8. The debate about crack baby syndrome will be discussed in detail in the next chapter.
9. Reeves and Campbell, *Crack coverage,* 208.

10. *Washington Post,* December 5, 1989, August 6, 1989; *New York Times,* May 7, 1989.

11. Reeves and Campbell, *Crack coverage,* 209.

12. *Roe v. Wade* is the 1973 Supreme Court ruling that legalized abortion. See Solinger, R., *Wake up little Susie: Single pregnancy and race before Roe v. Wade* (New York: Routledge, 2000).

13. Ibid., 24. See also U.S. Congress, House, District of Columbia Committee, *Investigation of public school conditions: Hearings before the Special Subcommittee to Investigate Public School Standards and Conditions and Juvenile Delinquency in the District of Columbia,* September 19 and October 1, 1956 (84th Cong., 2d sess.) (Washington , D.C: Government Printing Office, 1956), cited in Solinger, *Wake up little Susie.*

14. Solinger, *Wake up little Susie,* 24; *Richmond News Leader,* March 22, 1957, cited in Solinger.

15. Reeves and Campbell, *Crack coverage,* 210.

16. Chasnoff, I. J., Landress, H. J., and Barrett, M., The prevalence of illegal drug or alcohol use during pregnancy and discrepancies in mandatory reporting in Pinellas County, Florida, *New England Journal of Medicine, 322* (1990), 1202–6; Mathias, R., Women and drug abuse: NIDA survey provides first national data on drug use during pregnancy, *NIDA Notes, 1* (1995), 1.

17. Ibid.

18. Besharov, D., Crack children in foster care, *Children Today, 19* (1990), 21–25.

19. Ibid.; National Institute of Justice, *Drug Use Forecasting Annual Report* (Washington, D.C.: Government Printing Office, 1990).

20. Katz, M., *The undeserving poor: From the war on poverty to the war on welfare* (New York: Pantheon Books, 1989).

21. Joffe, C., Welfare reform and reproductive politics on a collision course: Contradictions in the conservative agenda. In Lo, C. Y. H., and Schwartz, M. (eds.), *Social policy and the conservative agenda,* 290–301 (Malden, Mass.: Blackwell, 1998).

22. Murray, C., *Losing ground: American social policy, 1950–1980* (New York: Basic Books, 1984). Also see Joffe, Welfare reform.

23. Ibid.

24. Greenstein, R. (1988). *Holes in Safety Net Programs and Policies in the States.* Washington, D.C.: Center on Budget and Policy Priorities.

25. Weicher, J., *Entitlement issues in the domestic budget: The long-term agenda* (Washington, D.C.: American Enterprise Institute for Public Policy Research, 1985).

26. Humphries, D., *Crack mothers: Pregnancy, drugs, and the media* (Columbus: Ohio State University Press, 1999).

27. Caring for crack/cocaine-exposed infants is estimated to have added more than $500 million a year nationally to the cost of normal labor, delivery and newborn care in 1990. See Scott, G., High Cost of Crack Babies, *News Monitor,* November 1991, 1.

28. *Christian Science Monitor,* February 15, 1989; *New York Times,* May 10 and August 7, 1989; and *Time,* May 13, 1991.

29. Reeves and Campbell, *Crack coverage.*

30. Chasnoff, Landress, and Barrett, The prevalence of illegal drug or alcohol use during pregnancy.

31. Roberts, D., Unshackling Black motherhood, *Michigan Law Review, 95* (1997), 938–64. Also refer to Paltrow, L., Defending the rights of pregnant addicts, *Champion,* August 1993, 18–19.

32. Paltrow, L. M., Cohen, D. S., and Carey, C. A., *Governmental responses to pregnant women who use alcohol or other drugs* (Washington, D.C.: Women's Law Project, 2000).

33. Moss, K. L., Paltrow, L., and Crockett, J., *Women's rights project* (Washington, D.C.: American Civil Liberties Union, 1990).

34. Ibid.

35. Chavkin, W., Help Don't Jail Addicted Mothers, *New York Times,* August, 1989, p. A-21; Chavkin, W., Testimony before the House Select Committee on Children, Youth and Families, U.S. House of Representatives, April, 27, 1989.

36. Kusserow, R. P., *Crack babies,* Report of the Office of the Inspector General (Washington, D.C.: Department of Health and Human Services, 1990).

37. U.S. Department of Health and Human Services, *National study of protective, preventive, and reunification services delivered to children and their families* (Washington, D.C.: Government Printing Office, 1997).

38. Jones, R. L., McCollough, C., and Dewoody, M. The child welfare challenge in meeting developmental needs, in *Identifying the needs of drug-affected children: Public policy issues*, 109–29 (Washington, D.C.: U.S. Department of Health and Human Services, 1992).

39. Feig, L., Understanding the problem: The gap between substance abuse programs and child welfare services, in Hampton, R. L., Senatore, V., and Gullotta, T. P. (eds.), *Substance abuse, family violence, and child welfare: Bridging perspectives*, 62–95 (London: Sage Publications, 1998).

40. Ibid.

41. Gregorie, T. K., Assessing the benefits and increasing the utility of addiction training for child welfare workers: A pilot study, *Child Welfare*, 73, 1 (1994), 69–81; Tracey, E. M., Maternal substance abuse: Protecting the child, preserving the family, *Social Work*, 39, 5 (1994), 534–40.

42. Humphries, *Crack mothers*.

43. U.S. Department of Health and Human Services, Office of the Assistant Secretary for Planning and Evaluation, *A review of family preservation and family reunification programs* (Washington, D.C.: Government Printing Office, 1995).

44. Center for Reproductive Law and Policy, In the courts: Ferguson v. City of Charleston, available at http://www.crlp.org/crt_preg_ferguson.html.

45. Ibid.

46. States that have adopted such laws includes Florida, Illinois, Indiana, Iowa, Maryland, Minnesota, Nevada, New York, Oklahoma, Rhode Island, South Carolina, Texas, Utah, and Wisconsin. For a more detailed discussion, refer to Paltrow, Cohen, and Carey, *Governmental responses*.

47. Personal Responsibility and Work Opportunity Reconciliation Act of 1996, Public Law 104–193. This law applies to those with convictions after August 22, 1996.

48. Amnesty International, *Not part of my sentence: Violations of the human rights of women in custody* (Washington, D.C.: Amnesty International, 1999), 26; Federal Bureau of Investigation, *Uniform crime reports 1985* (Washington, D.C.: Government Printing Office, 1986), 181, table 37; Federal Bureau of Investigation, *Uniform crime reports 1997* (Washington, D.C.: Government Printing Office, 1998), 231, table 42; National Advocates for Pregnant Women, http:// advocatesforpregnantwomen.org.

49. Greenfield, L. A., and Snell, T. L., *Bureau of Justice statistics, women offenders* (Washington, D.C.: Department of Justice, 1999), 5, table 11; National Advocates for Pregnant Women, http://advocatesforpregnantwomen.org.

50. Irwin, J., Schiraldi, V., and Ziedenberg, J., *America's one million nonviolent prisoners* (Washington, D.C.: Justice Policy Institute, 1999), 6–7; National Advocates for Pregnant Women, http://advocatesforpregnantwomen.org.

51. National Center on Addiction and Substance Abuse Services at Columbia University, *Substance abuse and women on welfare* (New York: National Center, 1996); U.S. Department of Health and Human Services, Office of the Assistant Secretary for Planning and Evaluation, *Patterns of substance use and substance-related impairments among participants in Aid to Families with Dependent Children Program (AFDC)* (Washington, D.C.: Government Printing Office, 1994).

52. Paltrow, Cohen, and Carey, *Governmental responses*.

53. U.S. Department of Health and Human Services, Office of the Assistant Secretary for Planning and Evaluation, *Patterns of substance use;* U.S. Department of Health and Human Services, Office of the Assistant Secretary for Planning and Evaluation, *Patterns of substance abuse and program participation* (Washington, D.C.: Government Printing Office, 1994).

54. Allard, P., *Life sentences: Denying welfare benefits to women convicted of drug-related offenses* (Washington, D.C.: The Sentencing Project, 2002).

55. Ibid.

56. Ibid.

57. Ibid.

58. Ibid.

59. Ibid.

60. Administration for Children and Families, Department of Health and Human Services, *The Adoption and Foster Care Analysis and Reporting System—Data for the Period Ending March 31, 1999* (Washington, D.C.: Government Printing Office, 2000).

61. Ibid.

62. United States General Accounting Office, *Foster Care: HHS Could Better Facilitate the Interjurisdictional Adoption Process* (Washington, D.C.: Government Printing Office, 1999).

63. Humphries, *Crack mothers.*
64. Drug Strategies, *Keeping Score 1998 Center for Substance Abuse Treatment*; Vivian D. Brown, Interview with Maggie Wilmore, Chief of Women and Children's Branch, Center for Substance Abuse Treatment. Journal of Psychoactive Drugs, 1995, 27 (4) 321–323; *SAMHSA Funding for Women-Specific Programs.* Substance Abuse and Mental Health Services Administration, 1995.
65. Mechanic, D., Schlesinger, M., and McAlpine, D. D., Management of mental health and substance abuse services: State of the art and early results, *The Milbank Quarterly, 73* (1995), 19–55.
66. Substance Abuse and Mental Health Services Administration, National Clearinghouse for Drug and Alcohol Information. (1999). *The Costs and Benefits of Substance Abuse Treatment: Findings from the National Treatment Improvement Evaluation Study,* 1999, available online at http://neds.calib.com/products/pdfs/cost-ben.pdf.
67. Most drug-abusing pregnant women are polydrug users—mixing a combination of substances. This issue will be discussed in more detail in the next chapter.
68. For a more detailed discussion, see Galanter, M., Keller, D. S., Dermatis, H., and Egelko, S. The impact of managed care on substance abuse treatment: A report of the American Society of Addiction Medicine, *Journal of Addictive Diseases,* 19, 3 (2000), 27. Also see Grumbach, K., Osmond, D., Vranizan, K., Jaffe, D., and Bindman, A.B. Primary care physicians' experience of financial incentives in managed care systems, *New England Journal of Medicine, 339 (21)* (1998), 1516–21.
69. State of Florida Agency for Health Care Administration, *Drug abuse hospitalization cost study,* 1999, available online at http://www.fdhc.state.fl.us/index.shtml.
70. Dace, S., et. al., Cost-effectiveness for drug-abusing pregnant women, *Drug and Alcohol Dependence, 45* (1997), 105–13.
71. This is a slogan used by the C.R.A.C.K. organization. It has been quoted in several related articles. Some include:
    "Mothers Paid to Stop Having children," *Marie Claire,* December 1998.
    "Controversial 'cash-for-sterilization' California group comes to New York: Critics Say 'C.R.A.C.K.' perpetuates misinformation and prejudice. *National Advocates for Pregnant Women Press Release* October 7, 2002.
    Children or Crack: Which Would You Choose? *Family Watch Library, Source:* London, December 1998.
    "Controversial Cash-for-Birth-Control Comes to Baltimore" *Baltimore City Paper,* April 18–24, 2001.
    "Cracking open CRACK: Unethical Sterilization Movement Gains Momentum" *Different Takes,* A Publication of the Population and Development Program At Hampshire College. Spring 2000. No. 2.
    "*Putting A price Tag on An addict's Womb*" Los Vegas Weekly, September 24, 2003.
72. Ibid.
73. United States Department of Health and Human Services, National Center on Child Abuse and Neglect, *A report on child maltreatment in alcohol-abusing families* (Washington, D.C.: Government Printing Office, 1993).
74. Ibid.
75. Ibid.
76. This will be discussed in detail in the next chapter.
77. The Committee on Women, Population and the Environment, *Crack uses unethical tactics to stop women with substance abuse problems from becoming pregnant,* http://advocatesfor pregnantwomen.org; Scully, J. M. (2000). *Cracking Open CRACK: Unethical Sterilization Movement Gains Momentum.* National Coalition Against CRACK; The National Coalition Against C.R.A.C.K., *The CRACK program: Discriminatory, unethical, ineffective and bad public policy,* http://www.cwpe.org/issues/health_html/contraceptives/crack/cac_factsheet. html.
78. The Committee on Women, population and the Environment, *Crack uses unethical tactics to stop women with substance abuse problems from becoming pregnant;* The National Coalition Against CRACK, The CRACK program.
79. Scully, J. M. (2000). *Cracking Open CRACK.*
80. Ibid.

81. Ibid.
82. Ibid.; National Coalition Against C.R.A.C.K., *The Crack Program.*
83. This will also be discussed in the next chapter.
84. Belenko, S. R., *Crack and the evolution of the anti-drug policy* (London: Greenwood Press, 1993).
85. Rydell, C. P., and Everingham, S. S., *Controlling cocaine,* report prepared for the Office of National Drug Control Policy and the United States Army (Santa Monica: Drug Policy Research Center, Rand Corporation, 1994).

Chapter 2

1. Trost, C., As drug babies grow older, schools strive to meet their needs, *Wall Street Journal,* December 29, 1989, A1–A2.
2. Elliott, K. T., and Coker, D. R., Crack babies: Here they come, ready or not, *Journal of Instructional Psychology, 18* (1991), 60–64; Rist, M. C., "Crack babies" in school, *Education Digest, 55* (1990), 30–33; Chira, S., Crack babies turn 5 and schools brace, *New York Times,* May 5, 1990; Highley, S., "Crack babies" in the classroom, *Journal of Instructional Psychology, 18* (1991), 208–10.
3. Greer, J. V., The drug babies, *Exceptional Children, 56* (1990), 382–84. Also see Poulsen, L. V., Cole, C., Woodruff, G., and Griffith, D., *Born substance exposed, educationally vulnerable* (Reston, Va.: The Council for Exceptional Children, 1991); Rist, M. C., The shadow children, *American School Board Journal, 177, 1* (1990), 18–24.
4. Laderman, D. A., Crack babies: Ready or not, here they come. *American Teacher, 75, 930* (1990), 9–16.
5. The term "crack baby syndrome" is not necessarily used in medical journals. It is used throughout this chapter to represent the all the conditions in children resulting from crack exposure.
6. Frank, D. A., Augustyn, M., Grant, W., Knight, W. G., Tripler, P., and Zuckerman, B., Growth, development, and behavior in early childhood following prenatal cocaine exposure, *Journal of the American Medical Association, 285, 12* (2001), 1–33.
7. Ibid., 1.
8. Ibid.
9. Acker, D., Sachs, B. P., Tracey, K. J., and Wise, W. E., Abruptio placentae associated with cocaine use, *American Journal of Obstetrics and Gynecology, 2* (1983), 220–21; Baxter, A., Butler, L. S., Brinkler, R. P., Frazier, W. A., and Wedgeworth, D. M., Effective early intervention for children prenatally exposed to cocaine in an inner-city context, in Lewis, M., and Bendersky, M. (eds.), *Mothers, babies, and cocaine: The role of toxins in development,* 335–53 (Hillsdale, N.J.: Lawrence Erlbaum and Associates, 1995).
10. Chasnoff, I. J., Burns, W. J., Schnoll, S. H., and Burns, K. A., Cocaine use in pregnancy, *New England Journal of Medicine, 331* (1985), 666–69.
11. Ibid.
12. Bauchner, H., Zuckerman, B., McCain, M., Frank, D., Fried, L. E., and Kane, H., Risk of sudden infant death syndrome among infants with in utero exposure to cocaine, *Journal of Pediatrics, 113* (1988), 831–34; Chasnoff, I. J., Bussy, M. E., Savich, R., and Stack, C. M., Perinatal cerebral infarction and maternal cocaine use, *Journal of Pediatrics, 108* (1986), 456–59; Chasnoff, I. J., Lewis, D. E., Griffith, D. R., and Willey, S., Cocaine and pregnancy: Clinical and toxicological implications for neonate, *Clinical Chemistry, 35, 7* (1989), 1276–8; Chasnoff, I. J., Cocaine, pregnancy and the neonate, *Women's Health, 15* (1989), 23–25; Chasnoff, I. J., and Griffith, D. R., Cocaine: Clinical studies of pregnancy and the newborn, *Annuals of the New York Academy of Sciences, 562* (1989), 260–66; Chasnoff, I. J., Hunt, C. E., Kletter, R., and Kaplan, D., Prenatal cocaine exposure is associated with respiratory pattern abnormalities, *American Journal of Diseases of Children, 143* (1989), 583–587; Dixon, S. S., Coen, R. W., and Crutchfield, W., Visual dysfunction in cocaine exposed infants, *Pediatric Research, 21* (1987), 359A; Fulroth, R., Phillips, B., and Durand, D., Perinatal outcome of infants exposed to cocaine and/or heroin in utero, *American Journal of Diseases of Children, 43* (1989), 905–10; Kelley, S. J., Walsh, J. H., and Thompson, K. (1991), Birth outcomes, health problems, and neglect with prenatal cocaine exposure to cocaine, *Pediatric Nurse, 17* (1989), 130–36; Little, B. B., Snell, L. M., Klein, V. R., and Gilstrap, L. C. III, Cocaine abuse during pregnancy: maternal and fetal implications, *Obstetrics and*

Gynecology, 73 (1989), 157–60; Madden, J. D., Payne, T. F., and Miller, S., Maternal cocaine abuse and effect on the newborn, *Pediatrics 77* (1986), 209–11; MacGregor, S. N., Keith, L. G., Chasnoff, I. J., Rosner, M. A., Chisum, G. M., Shaw, P., and Minogue, J. P., Cocaine use during pregnancy: Adverse perinatal outcome, *American Journal of Obstetrics and Gynecology, 157* (1987), 686–90; Oro, A. S., and Dixon, S. D., Perinatal cocaine and methamphetamine exposure: Maternal and neonatal correlates, *Journal of Pediatrics, 111* (1987), 571–79; Riley, J. G., and Porat, R., Abnormal pneumograms in infants with in utero cocaine exposure, *Pediatric Research, 21* (1987), 262A; Wilson, G. S., Clinical studies of infants and children exposed prenatally to heroin, *Annals of the New York Academy of Sciences, 562* (1989), 183–94; Zuckerman, B., Frank, D. A., Hingson, R., Amaro, H., Levenson, S. M., Kayne, H., Parker, S., Vinci, R., Aboagye, K., Fried, L. E., et al., Effects of marijuana and cocaine use on fetal growth, *New England Journal of Medicine, 320* (1989), 762–68.

13. Goodman, E., The myth of the "crack babies," *Boston Globe,* January 12, 1992, 69; Besharov, D. J., Crack babies: The worst threat is mom herself, *Washington Post,* August 6, 1989. Also see Tanner, L., Worries about "crack babies" are exaggerated, *Chicago Sun-Times,* March 28, 2001.

14. Mayes, L. C., Granger, R. H., Bornstein, M. H., and Zuckerman, B., The problem of prenatal cocaine exposure: A rush to judgment, *Journal of the American Medical Association, 267* (1992), 406–8.

15. Inciardi, J. A., Lockwood, D., and Pottieger, A. E., *Women and crack cocaine* (New York: Macmillan, 1993); Murphy, S., and Rosenbaum, M., *Pregnant women on drugs: Combating stereotypes and stigma* (New Brunswick: Rutgers University Press, 1999); Humphries, D., *Crack mothers: Pregnancy, drugs and the media* (Columbus: Ohio State University Press, 1999).

16. See Mayes et al., The problem with prenatal cocaine exposure.

17. Chasnoff, I. J., Griffith, D. R., Freier, C., and Murry, J., Cocaine/polydrug use in pregnancy: Two-year follow-up, *Pediatrics, 89* (1992), 284–89; Griffith, D. R., Azuma, S. D., and Chasnoff, I. J., Three-year outcome of children exposed prenatally to drugs, *Journal of the American Academy of Child and Adolescent Psychiatry, 33, 1* (1994), 20–34; Hurt, H., Brodsky, N. L., Betancourt, L., Braitman, L. E., Malmud, E., and Gianetta, J., Cocaine exposed children: Follow-up through 30 months, *Journal of Developmental Behavioral Pediatrics, 16* (1995), 29–35; Hurt, H., Brodsky, N. L., Braitman, L. E., and Gianetta, J., Natal status of infants of cocaine users and control subjects: A prospective comparison, *Journal of Perinatology, 15, 4* (1995), 297–304; Hurt, H., A prospective evaluation of early language development in children with in utero cocaine exposure and in control subjects, *Journal of Pediatrics, 130* (1997), 310–12; Lutiger, B., Graham, K., Einarson, T. R., and Koren, G., Relationship between gestational cocaine use and pregnancy outcome, *Teratology, 44* (1991), 405–14; McCalla, S., Minkoff, H. L., and Feldman, J., The biologic and social consequences of perinatal cocaine use in an inner-city population. Results of an anonymous cross-sectional study, *American Journal of Obstetrics and Gynecology, 164* (1991), 625–30; Zuckerman et al., Effects of maternal marijuana and cocaine use on fetal growth.

18. Griffith, D., Azuma, S. D., and Chasnoff, I. J., Three-year outcome of children prenatally exposed to drugs, *Journal of the American Academy of Child and Adolescent Psychiatry, 33, 1* (1994), 20–27.

19. Ibid. The Stanford-Binet Intelligence Scale is a standardized test that assesses intelligence and cognitive abilities in children.

20. Hurt et al., (1995). *Cocaine exposed children.* The Bayley Scales of Infant Development measure mental, physical, social, and emotional development. The Bayley Scales are often used to determine whether a child is developing normally and to provide an early diagnosis for intervention in the case of developmental delay.

21. Chasnoff et al., Cocaine/polydrug use in pregnancy.

22. This issue will be discussed in further detail in the next chapter.

23. This issue will be discussed in further detail in the next chapter.

24. This issue will be discussed in further detail in the next chapter.

25. Napiorkowski, B., Lester, B. M., Freier, M. C., Brunner, S., Dietz, L., Nadra, A., and Oh, W., Effects of in utero substance exposure on infant neurobehavior, *Pediatrics 98, 1* (1996), 71–75.

26. The NICU Network Neurobehavioral Scale was developed for the National Intensive Child Health and Human Development Neonatal Research Network as part of a multisite clinical trial of the effects of prenatal drug exposure on child outcome (see Napiorkowski et al., Effects of in utero substance exposure).

27. Napiorkowski et al., Effects of in utero substance exposure.
28. Arendt, R., Angelopoulos, J., Salvator, A., and Singer, L., Motor development of cocaine-exposed children at age two years, *Pediatrics, 103* (1999), 86–92.
29. Richardson, G. A., Hamel, S. C., Goldschmidt, L., and Day, N. L., Growth of infants prenatally exposed to cocaine/crack: Comparison of a prenatal care and a no prenatal care sample, *Pediatrics, 104, 2* (1999), 1e18.
30. Richardson, G. A., Prenatal cocaine exposure: A longitudinal study of development, in Harvey, J. A., and Kosofsky, B. E. (eds.), *Cocaine: Effects on the developing brain,* 144–52:e18 (New York: New York Academy of Sciences, 1998).
31. Mayes, L. C., Grillon, C., Granger, R., and Schottenfeld, R., Regulation of arousal and attention in preschool children exposed prenatally to cocaine, in Harvey, J. A., and Kosofsky, B. E. (eds.), *Cocaine: Effects on the developing brain,* 126–43 (New York: New York Academy of Sciences, 1998).
32. Chasnoff, I. J., Anson, A., Hatcher, R., Stenson, H., Iaukea, K., and Randolph, L. A., Prenatal exposure to cocaine and other drugs: Outcome at 4 to 6 years, in Harvey, J. A., and Kosofsky, B. E. (eds.), *Cocaine: Effects on the developing brain,* 314–28 (New York: New York Academy of Sciences, 1998). Also see Chasnoff, I. J., Anson, A. R., and Iaukea, K. A., Understanding the drug-exposed child: Approaches to behavior and learning (Chicago: Imprint Publications, 1998).
33. Lu, N. T., Taylor, B. G., and Riley, K. J., The validity of adult arrestee self- reports of crack cocaine use, *American Journal of Drug and Alcohol Abuse, 27, 3* (2001), 399–419.
34. Day, N. L., and Robles, N., Methodological issues in the measurement of substance abuse, *Annals of the New York Academy of Sciences, 562* (1989), 8–13.
35. Ibid.
36. Howard, J., and Beckwith, L., Issues in subject recruitment and retention with pregnant and parent substance-abusing women, in Rahdert, E. (ed.), *Treatment for drug-exposed women and their children: Advances in research methodology,* 69–85 (Rockville, Md.: U.S. Department of Health and Human Services, 1996).
37. Ostrea, E. M., Brady, M., Gausse, S., Raymundo, A. L., and Stevens, M., Drug screening of newborns by meconium analysis. A large scale prospective, epidemiologic study, *Pediatrics, 111* (1992), 571–78; Ostrea, E. M., Lizardo, E., and Tanafranca, M., The prevalence of illicit drug exposure in the NICU as determined by meconium drug screen, *Pediatric Research, 31* (1992), 215A.
38. Frank, D. A., Zuckerman, B. S., Amaro, H., Aboague, K., Bauchner, H., Cabral, H., et al., Cocaine use during pregnancy: Prevalence and correlates, *Pediatrics, 82* (1988), 888–95; Matera, C., Warren, W. B., Moomjy, M., Fink, D. J., and Fox, H. E., Prevalence of cocaine use and other substances in an obstetric population, *American Journal of Obstetrics and Gynecology, 163* (1990), 797–801; Garcia, D. C., Romero, A., Garcia, G. C., and Ostrea, E. M., Gastric fluid analysis for determining gestational cocaine exposure, *Pediatrics, 98* (1996), 291–93.
39. Evan B. Donaldson Adoption Institute, *Adoption and prenatal alcohol and drug exposure: Implications for adoption practice,* 1997, available at http://www.adoptioninstitute.org/proed/pserjw10.html.
40. Singer, L. T., Arendt, R., Minnes, S., Farkas, K., Salvator, A., Kirchner, H. L., and Kliegman, R., Cognitive and motor outcomes of cocaine exposed infants, *Journal of the American Medical Association, 287* (2002), 1–19.
41. Ibid., 9.
42. Halstead, A. C., Godolphin, W., Lickitch, G., and Segal, S., Timing of specimen collection is crucial in urine screening of drug-dependent mothers and newborns, *Clinical Biochemistry, 21* (1988), 59–61; Lester, B. M., Freier, K., and LaGasse, L. L., Prenatal cocaine exposure and child outcome: What do we really know? in Lewis, M., and Bendersky, M. (eds.), *Mothers, babies, and cocaine: The role of toxins in development,* 19–39 (Hillsdale, N.J.: Lawrence Erlbaum Associates, 1995).
43. Kwong, T. C., and Ryan, R. M., Detection of intrauterine illicit drug exposure by newborn drug testing, *Clinical Chemistry, 43* (1997), 235–42.
44. Ibid.; Blank, D. L., and Kidwell, D. A., Decontamination procedures for drugs of abuse in hair: Are they sufficient? *Forensic Science International, 70* (1995),13–38; Wang, W. L., and Cone, E. J., Testing human hair for drugs of abuse. IV. Environmental cocaine contamination and washing effects, *Forensic Science International, 70* (1995), 39–51; Bailey, D. N., Drug screening in an unconventional matrix: Hair analysis, *Journal of the American Medical Association, 262* (1989), 331.

45. Halstead, A. C., Godolphin, W., Lockitch, G., and Segal, S., Timing of specimen is crucial in urine of drug dependent mothers and infants, *Clinical Biochemistry, 21* (1988), 59–61.
46. Ostrea, E. M., Meconium drug analysis, Mectest Corporation Document 5889, Rowland Heights, Calif., 1996.
47. Ibid.; Ostrea, E. M., Parks, P., and Brady, M., Rapid isolation and detection of drugs in meconium of infants of drug dependent mothers, *Clinical Chemistry, 34* (1988), 2372–3.
48. Ostrea, E. M. and others (1988). Rapid isolation and deletion of drugs in meconium of infants of dependent mothers; Ostrea, E. M. (1996). Meconium drug analysis.
49. Ostrea, E. M., Brady, M. J., Parks, P. M., Asensio, D. C., and Naluz, A., Drug screening of meconium in infants of drug dependent mothers: An alternative to urine testing, *Journal of Pediatrics, 115* (1989), 474–77; Maynard, E. C., Amuroso, L. P., and Oh, W., Meconium for drug testing, *American Journal of Diseases of Children, 145* (1991), 650–52; Callahan, C. M., Grant, T. M., Phillips, P., Clark, G., et al., Measurement for gestational cocaine exposure: Sensitivity of newborn: hair, meconium and urine, *Journal of Pediatrics, 120* (1992), 763–68; Ostrea, E. M., Brady, M., Gausse, S., et al., Drug screening of newborns by meconium analysis: A large scale, prospective, epidemiological study, *Pediatrics, 89* (1992), 107; Bandstra, E. S., Stele, B. W., Chitwood, D. D., et al., Detection of in utero cocaine exposure: a comparative methodologic study, *Pediatric Research, 31* (1992), 58A.
50. Sinclair, E., Head Start children at risk: Relationship of prenatal drug use, identification of special needs and subsequent special education placement, *Journal of Behavioral Disorders, 23, 2* (1998), 125–33.
51. Delaney-Black, V., Covington, C., Templin, T., Ager, J., Martier, S., and Sokol, R., Prenatal cocaine exposure and child behavior, *Pediatrics, 102, 4* (1998), 945–50.
52. Delaney-Black, V., Covington, C., Templin, T., Ager, J., Nordstorm-Klee, B., Martier, S., Leddick, L., Czerwinski, R. H., and Skokol, R. J., Teacher assessed behavior of children prenatally exposed to cocaine, *Pediatrics, 106, 4* (2000), 782–91.
53. Waller, M. B., Crack babies grown up, *American School Board Journal, 181* (1994), 30–31.
54. Ibid., 30.
55. Lester, B. M., LaGasse, L. L., and Seifer, R., Cocaine exposure and children: The meaning of subtle effects, *Science, 282* (1998), 633–34.
56. Ibid., 633.

Chapter 3

1. Schipper, W., *Drug-exposed children in the schools*: Problems and policy, Testimony before the U.S. House of Representatives Select Committee on Narcotics Abuse and Control (Washington, D.S.: Government Printing Office, 1991).
2. Ibid.
3. Early Intervention Programs for Infants and Toddlers with Disabilities, Part C of the Individuals with Disabilities Education Act (IDEA), 20 U.S.C. Chapter 33, Section 1431, as amended by Public Law 105–17. This legislation had its origins in Public Law 94–142, the Education for All Handicapped Children Act.
4. The age range and name for this program varies from state to state. It is variously referred to as the Infants and Toddlers with Disabilities Education Act, zero-to-two, zero-to-three, or birth-to-three.
5. Stayton, TK, and Karnes, TK, Model programs for infants and toddlers, in Johnson, L. J., Gallagher, R. J., LaMontagne, M. J., Jordan, J. B., Gallagher, J. J., Huntinger, P. L., and Karnes, M. B. (eds.), *Meeting Early Intervention Challenges: Issues from Birth to Three,* 34 (Baltimore: Paul H. Brookes, 1994).

   Also see table 1 on page 238 in Gallagher, J. J., Harbin, G., Eckland, J., and Clifford, R., State diversity and policy implementation: Infants and toddlers, in the same volume.
6. Schipper, W., (1991). *Drug-exposed children in the schools.*
7. Ibid.
8. Gallagher et al., State diversity and policy implementation.
9. Ibid.
10. Danaher, J., *Part C updates* (Chapel Hill: National Early Childhood Technical Assistance Center, University of North Carolina, 2002), 36.
11. Gallagher et al., State diversity and policy implementation.

12. Ibid.,. 240–41.
13. Danaher, *Part C updates,* 36.
14. Harbin, G. L., and Maxwell, K., *Progress toward developing a definition for developmentally delayed: Report #2* (Chapel Hill: Carolina Policy Studies Program, University of North Carolina, 1991); Harbin, G. L., and Terry, D., *Definition of developmentally delayed and at-risk infants and toddlers* (Chapel Hill: Carolina Policy Studies Program, University of North Carolina, 1990). Also see Harbin, G. L., Gallagher, J. J., and Terry, D. V., Defining the eligible population: Policy issues and challenges, *Journal of Early Intervention, 15, 1* (1990), 13–20.
15. House Committee Report, H.R. 1013, 34, cited in "Educational policy issues in serving infants and toddlers born toxic positive to cocaine," in Quinton, S. L., Johnson, S. A., Johnson, E. M., Denniston, R. W., and Auguston, K. L. (eds.), *Identifying the needs of drug-affected children: Public policy issues,* OSAP Prevention Monograph 11, publication 3 ADM 92–1814, 133–38 (Rockville, Md.: Office for Substance Abuse Prevention, U.S. Department of Health and Human Services, 1992).
16. Gallagher et al., State diversity and policy implementation.
17. Ibid.
18. Schipper, *Drug-exposed children in the schools.*
19. Gallagher et al., State diversity and policy implementation.
20. Ibid.
21. Smith, TK, and McKenna, TK, Early intervention and public policy, in Johnson, L. J., Gallagher, R. J., LaMontagne, M. J., Jordan, J. B., Gallagher, J. J., Huntinger, P. L., and Karnes, M. B. (eds.), *Meeting early intervention challenges,* 251–64 (Baltimore: Paul H. Brookes, 1994).
22. Trohanis, P. L., *Progress in providing services to young children with special needs and their families: An overview to and updates on the implementation of the Individuals with Disabilities Education Act (IDEA),* NECTAC Notes no. 12 (Chapel Hill: FPG Child Development Institute, National Early Childhood Technical Assistance Center, University of North Carolina at Chapel Hill, 2002), 2.
23. Ibid., 4.
24. Danaher, *Part C updates.*
25. Ibid.
26. Special ed. services in Ill. fall short, judge rules, *Education Week,* February 14, 1996; Judge: Illinois "dragging its feet" on part H services, *The Special Educator, 11, 15* (1996).
27. Ibid.
28. Trohanis, *Progress in providing services.*
29. McNeil, J., *Americans with disabilities, 1991–1992: Data from the survey of income and program participation,* Current Population Reports, 70–73 (Washington, D.C.: U.S. Department of Commerce, Bureau of the Census, 1993), cited in Bowe, F. G., Population estimates: Birth to 5 children with disabilities, *Journal of Special Education, 28, 4* (1995), 461–71.
30. Bowe, Population estimates. The author noted that some of these children received services through other programs, which, while similar to the IDEA, were not necessarily provided by Title I elementary and secondary programs.
31. Danaher, J., *Eligibility policies and practices for young children under Part B of the IDEA,* NECTAC Notes no. 9 (Chapel Hill: FPG Child Development Institute, National Early Childhood Technical Assistance Center, University of North Carolina at Chapel Hill, 2001).
32. Reauthorization of disability-related legislation, 103rd Cong., 1st Sess. (March 10, 1994). Also cited in Humphries, D., *Crack mothers: Pregnancy, drugs and the media* (Columbus: Ohio State University Press, 1999).
33. Danaher, J., *Eligibility policies and practices,* 2.
34. Ibid.
35. Trohanis, *Progress in providing services,* 2.
36. Ibid.
37. Ibid., 3.
38. Ibid.
39. Ibid., 4.
40. Humphries, *Crack mothers.* 1999.
41. This will be discussed in more detail in the chapter on teachers' observations.
42. Chasnoff, I. J., Hope for a lost generation, *School Safety,* winter 1992, 4–6.
43. Ibid.

44. Brady, J. P., Posner, M., Lang, C., and Rosati, M. J., *Risk and reality: The implications of prenatal exposure to alcohol and other drugs* (n.p.: The Education Development Center, 1994); Sautter, C. R., Crack: Healing the children, *Phi Delta Kappan, 74* (1992), K1–K12; Powell, D., *Elemplary programs serving young children prenatally exposed to drugs* (Washington, D.C.: Government Printing Office, 1991); Poulsen, M., *Schools meet the challenge: Educational needs of children at risk due to substance abuse*, Resources in Special Education (Sacramento, Calif.: Children's Resource Institute, 1992); Cole, C., Ferrara, V., Johnson, D., Jones, M., Schoenbaum, M., Tyler, R., Wallace, V., and Poulsen, M., *Today's challenge: Teaching strategies for working with young children prenatally exposed to drugs/alcohol* (Los Angeles CA: Los Angeles Unified School District, 1991).
45. Ibid.
46. Ibid.
47. Ibid.
48. Davis, E., *Testimony on Drug-Exposed Children. Hearing Before the Select Committee on Narcotic Abuse and Control* (Washington, D.C.: Government Printing Office, 1991); Sautter, Crack: Healing the children; Administration for Children and Families, *Head Start Family Service Center Demonstration Projects* (1994), 1–5.
49. Ibid.
50. Hime, G., Council for Exceptional Children, *Testimony before the U.S. Senate Committee on Labor and Human Resources concerning the Individuals with Disabilities Education Act*, January 29, 1997. Washington, D.C.: Government Printing Office.
51. Refer to the discussion in the previous chapter on the research on the developmental progress of drug-exposed children.
52. Individuals with Disabilities Education Act, Amendments of 1997.
53. Danaher, J., *Eligibility policies and practices.*
54. Ibid.
55. Ibid. Also see Shackelford, J., *Informed clinical opinion*, NECTAC Notes no. 10 (Chapel Hill: FPG Child Development Institute, National Early Childhood Technical Assistance Center, University of North Carolina, 2002).
56. Individuals with Disabilities Education Act, 1997, Final Regulations.
57. Parrish, T., *Disparities in the identification, funding, and provision of special education*, submitted to the Civil Rights Project for the Conference on Minority Issues in Special Education in Public Schools (Washington, D.C.: American Institutes for Research, 2000).
58. Ibid.
59. The quality of early intervention varies from program to program. See Hurley, D., Early childhood educators' beliefs and knowledge about the effects of prenatal exposure to alcohol, crack, cocaine, and a combination of substances on infants and young children, Ph.D. dissertation, Southern Illinois University, 1992; Chapman, J. K., and Elliott, R. N., Preschoolers exposed to cocaine: Early childhood special education and head start preparation, *Journal of Early Intervention, 19, 2* (1995), 118–29; Kim, Y. M., Sugai, G. M., and Kim, G., Early intervention needs of children at risk due to prenatal drug exposure: A survey of early childhood educators, *Journal of Research in Childhood Education, 13, 2* (1999), 207–15.
60. Hime, *Testimony*, 6–7.
61. Brotherson, M. J., Sheriff, G., Milburn, P., and Schertz, M., Elementary school principals and their needs and issues for inclusive early childhood education programs, *Topics in Early Childhood Education, 21, 1* (2001), 31–45.
62. Senate defeats special education funding measure, http://fyi.cnn.com/2001/fyi/teachers.ednews/05/18/special.education.ap/.
63. Democratic Party Committee, *The Bush Education Budget: Inadequate Resources for Reform*, http://democrats.senate.gov/~dpc/pubs/107–2-20.html.
64. Jacobson, L., and Bowman, D. H., Early-childhood-education advocates say president's budget fails to meet his rhetoric, *Education Week on the Web*, http://www.edweek.org/ew/newstory.cfm?slug=22budside1.h21.

Chapter 4

1. Whorton, J. E., Siders, J. A., Fowler, R. E., and Naylor, D. L., A two decade review of the number of students with disabilities receiving federal monies and the types of educational placements used, *Education, 121, 2* (2000), 287–97.

2. Ibid.
3. Clandinin, D. J., and Connelly, F. M., *Teacher professional knowledge landscapes* (New York: Teachers College Press, 1995); Foster, M., *Black teachers on teaching* (New York: New Press, 1999); Lasdon-Billings, G., *The dreamkeepers: Successful teachers of African-American children* (San Francisco: Jossey-Bass, 1994).
4. Connelly, F. M., and Clandinin, D. J., *Shaping a professional identity: Stories of educational practice* (New York: Teachers College Press, 1999).
5. Gitlin, A., and Russell, R., Alternative methodologies in the research context, in Gitlin, A. (ed)., *Power and Method*, 181–202 (London: Routledge, 1994).
6. Patton, M. Q., *Qualitative evaluation and research methods*, 2nd edition (Thousand Oaks, Calif.: Sage Publications, 1990), 230.
7. Research and Program Evaluation in Illinois: The extent and nature of drug and violent crime in Illinois counties, A profile of the Cook County Juvenile Justice System April 2000.
8. Ibid.
9. Concerns about DCFS raised. *The News-Gazette, (10/7/99)*.
10. Illinois Department of Children and Family Services.
11. Smart Steps: Treating Baltimore's Drug Problem. *http://www.drugstrategies.org/Baltimore/BltCh_l.html)*.
12. Ibid. Maryland Department of Health and Mental Hygiene, Alcohol and Drug Abuse Administration (ADAA). Based on treatment admission data for fiscal year (FY) 1998, ADAA estimated that 60,375 of Baltimore's residents will need treatment for substance abuse, amounting to 12.8 percent of the city's 471,147 adults in 1999, or 1 and 8 adults. ADAA acknowledges that this number could be much higher considering the number of people needing alcohol treatment and the number of criminal offenders needing substance abuse treatment. The number of Baltimore residents needing treatment may be in the range of 75,000 to 80,000. (see Smart Steps: Baltimore's Drug Problem, *http://www.drugstrategies. org/Baltimore/BltCh_l.html)*.
13. Shand. S. "Overdose deaths exceed slayings." *Baltimore Sun, (9/15/00)*.
14. Child Welfare League of America, Chemical Dependency Fact Sheet Drug Strategies. (1995). *Keeping Score: What we are getting for our federal drug control dollars.* Washington D.C.:
15. City schools must tackle special ed. *Baltimore Sun, (2/9/97)*.
16. Humphries, D., *Crack mothers: Pregnancy, drugs, and the media* (Columbus: Ohio State University Press, 1999), 144.
17. Merriam, S. B., *Qualitative research and case study applications in education* (San Francisco: Jossey-Bass, 1998).
18. This issue will be discussed in more detail in the section on social challenges.
19. This issue will be discussed in more detail in the section on social challenges.
20. The need for more specialized interventions is discussed in greater detail in the last chapter on policy implications.
21. Soby, J. M., *Prenatal exposure to drugs/alcohol: Characteristics and educational implications of fetal alcohol syndrome and cocaine/polydrug effects* (Springfield, Ill.: Charles C. Thomas, 1994).
22. Ibid.
23. The practice of full inclusion varies from district to district.
24. Essen, J., Lambert, L., and Head, J., School attainment of children who have been in care, *Child Care, Health and Development, 2* (1976), 339–51; Fanshel, D., and Shinn, E. B., *Children in foster care: A longitudinal investigation* (New York: Columbia University Press, 1978); Heath, A., Colton, M., and Aldgate, J., Educational progress of children in and out of care, *British Journal of Social Work, 19, 6* (1989); Jackson, S., Educating children in residential foster care, *Oxford Review of Education 20, 3* (1994), 267–80; Newton, R. R., Litrownik, A. J., and Landsverk, J. A., Children and youth in foster care: Detangling the relationship between problem behaviors and number of placements, *Child Abuse and Neglect, 24, 10* (2000), 1363–74.
25. Essen et al., School attainment.
26. Ibid.; Osborn, A., and St. Claire, L., The ability and behaviour of children who have been in care or separated from their parents, *Early Child Development and Care, 28, 3* (1987), 187–354.
27. The Care School is an alternative school in Champaign. It started out as just an alternative high school. Now there is a middle school for junior high students.
28. Allington, R. L., and McGill-Franzen, A., School response to reading failure: Instructions for chapter one and special education students grade two, four, and eight, *Elementary School Journal, 89* (1989), 529–42. Also see Hehir, T., Eliminating ableism in education, *Harvard Educational Review, 72, 1* (2002), 1–32.

29. Allington & McGill-Franzen, (1989). School response to reading failure. Heir, T. (2002). Eliminating ableism in education.

30. Special-ed teacher shortage racks city, *Chicago Tribune*, June 19, 2002; Many uncertified teachers work in worst schools: Credentials lacking in special ed too, *Chicago Tribune*, July 9, 2002; Hettleman, K. R., *Still getting it wrong: The continuing failure of special education in Baltimore city public schools* (Baltimore: Abell Foundation, 2002).

Chapter 5

1. Substance Abuse and Mental Health Services Administration, Office of Applied Studies, Women in treatment for smoked cocaine. Drug and Alcohol Services Information system report, July 13, 2001).

2. Ibid.

3. Ibid.

4. Forsyth, B., Leventhal, J., Qi, K., Johnson, L., Schroeder, D., and Votto, N., Health care and hospitalization of young children born to cocaine-using women, *Pediatrics and Adolescent Medicine, 152, 2* (1998), 177–84.

5. Chavkin, W., and Breitbart, V., Substance abuse and maternity: The United States as a case study, *Addiction, 92, 9* (1997), 1201–5.

6. Ibid.

7. Zellman, G. L., Jacobson, P. D., and Bell, R. M., Influencing physicians response to prenatal substance exposure through state legislation and work place practices, *Addiction, 92* (1997), 1123–31.

8. Chavkin, W., Breitbart, V., Elman, D. and Wise, P. H., National survey of the States: Policies and practices regarding drug-using pregnant women, *American Journal of Public Health, 88* (1998), 117–19; Chavkin, W., Wise, P. H., and Elman, D., Policies toward pregnancy and addiction: Sticks without carrots, in Harvey, J. A., and Kosofsky, B. E. (eds.), *Cocaine: Effects on the Developing Brain*, 335–40 (New York: New York Academy of Sciences, 1998).

9. Refer to the Chapter 3 discussion on drug-affected children and educational policies.

10. Danaher, J., *Part C updates* (Chapel Hill: National Early Childhood Technical Assistance Center, University of North Carolina, 2002)

11. Ibid.

12. Hurley, D., Early childhood educators' beliefs and knowledge about the effects of prenatal exposure to alcohol, crack, cocaine, and a combination of substances on infants and young children, Ph.D. dissertation, Southern Illinois University, 1992.

13. Chapman, J. K., and Elliott, R. N., Preschoolers exposed to cocaine: Early childhood special education and Head Start preparation, *Journal of Early Intervention, 19, 2* (1995), 118–29.

14. Pawl, J. H., Interventions to strengthen relationships between infants and drug-abusing or recovering parents, *Zero to Three, 13, 1* (1992), 6–10; Van Bremen, J. R., and Chasnoff, I. J., Policy issues for integrating parenting interventions and addiction treatment for women, *Topics in Early Childhood Special Education, 14, 2* (1994), 254–74; Harvey, C., Comfort, H. C., and Johns, N., Integrating parenting support into residential drug and alcohol treatment programs, *Zero to Three, 13, 1* (1992), 11–13.

15. Pawl, (1992). Interventions to strengthen relationships between infants and drug-abusing or recovering parents; Bremen & Chasnoff (1994). Policy issues for integrating parenting interventions; Comfort & Johns (1992), Integrating parenting support.

16. Ibid.

17. Ibid.

18. Merikangas, K., and Stevens, D. E., Substance abuse among women: Familial factors and comorbidity, in Wetherington, C. L., and Roman, A. B. (eds.), *Drug addiction research and the health of women* (Washington, D.C: National Institutes on Drug Abuse, 1998).; U.S. Department of Health and Human Services, Center for Substance Abuse Treatment, *Practical approaches in the treatment of women who abuse alcohol and other drugs* (Rockville, Md.: U.S. Dept. of Health and Human Services, Public Health Service, Substance Abuse and Mental Health Services Administration, Center for Substance Abuse Treatment, Division of Clinical Programs, Women and Children's Branch, 1994).

19. Cohen, F. S., and Denser-Gerber, J., A study of the relationship between child abuse and drug addiction in 178 patients: Preliminary results, *Child Abuse and Neglect, 6* (1982), 383–87.

20. Howard, J., Beckwith, L., Rodning, C., and Kropenska, V., The development of young children of substance-abusing parents: Insights from seven years of intervention and research, *Zero to Three, 9* (1989), 8–16; Baxter, A., Butler, L. S., Brinkler, R. P., Frazier, W. A., and Wedgeworth, D. M., Effective early intervention for children prenatally exposed to cocaine in an inner-city context, in Lewis, M., and Bendersky, M. (eds.), *Mothers, babies and cocaine: The role of toxins in development,* 335–53 (Hillsdale, N.J.: Lawrence Erlbaum Associates, 1995).

21. Ibid.

22. Heinicke, C. M., Beckwith, L., and Thompson, A., Early intervention in the family system: A framework and review, *Infant Mental Health Journal, 9* (1988), 111–41.

23. Ibid.

24. Leif, N. R., The drug user as a parent, *International Journal of Addictions, 20, 1* (1985), 63–97; U.S. Department of Health and Human Services, *Blending perspectives and building common ground: The complexity of child and family needs. A report to Congress on substance abuse and child protection* (Washington, D.C.: Government Printing Office, 1999).

25. Ibid.

26. Harvey, C., Comfort, M., and Johns, N. (1992). Integrating parent support into residential drug and alcohol treatment programs. *Zero to Three 13* (1), 11–13.

27. Statement of Gale Saler, deputy executive director, Second Genesis, Inc., Bethesda, Maryland. Testimony before The House Committee on Ways and Means Subcommittee on Human Resources, Hearing on Child Protection Issues, March 2000. Washington, D.C.: Government Printing Office.

28. Ibid.

29. Ibid.

30. Tracey, E., Maternal substance abuse: Protecting the child, preserving the family, *Social Work, 37, 5* (1994), 18–25; Hawley, T. L., Halle, T. G., Drasin, R. E., & Thomas, N. G. (1995). Children of addicted mothers: Effects of the "crack-epidemic" on the caregiving environment and the development of the preschooler. *American Journal of Orthopsychiatry, 63,* 364–379.

31. Wilson, B. L., Treatment for two, *Governing, 4, 10* (1991), 36–41; Haller, D. L., Recovery for two: Pregnancy and addiction, *Addiction and Recovery,* July/August 1991, 14–18.

32. Ibid.

33. Chasnoff, I. J., Anson, A. R., and Iaukea, K. A., Understanding the drug-exposed child: Approaches to behavior and learning (Chicago: Imprint Publications, 1998), 23.

34. Ibid.

35. Freier, M., Griffith, D., and Chasnoff, I., In utero drug exposure: Developmental follow-up and maternal infant interaction, *Seminars in Perinatology, 15* (1991), 310–16.

36. Delaney-Black, V., Covington, C., Templin, T., Ager, J., Martier, S., and Sokol, R., Prenatal exposure to cocaine and child behavior, *Pediatrics, 102, 4* (1998), 945–50.

37. Chasnoff et al., Understanding the drug-exposed child, 21.

38. Personal communication, June 27, 2002.

39. Ibid.

40. Powell, D. E., Educational interventions for substance exposed children now in preschool and kindergarten, in Puttkammer, C. H. (ed.), *Working with substance exposed children: Strategies for professionals* (Tucson: Therapy Skill Builders, 1994), 112.

41. Diane Powell, personal communication, July 7, 2002.

42. U.S. Department of Health and Human Services, Substance Abuse and Mental Health Services Administration, 1998 annual report to Congress on the evaluation of Comprehensive Community Mental Health Services for Children and Their Families program, 1999; U.S. Department of Health and Human Services, *Practical approaches.*

43. U.S. Department of Health and Human Services (1999). 1998 Annual Report to Congress on the Evaluation of Community Mental Health Services for Children. Washington, D.C.: Government Printing Office.

44. Ibid.

45. Manning, J. B., and Rodriguez, L., Community for learning: Connection with community services, in Wang, M. C., and Boyd, W. L. (eds.), *Improving results for children and families: Linking collaborative services with school reform efforts,* 19–33 (Greenwich, Conn.: Information Age Publishing, 2000).

46. Merseth, K. K., Schorr, L. B., and Elmore, R. F., Schools, community based interventions, and children's learning and development: What's the connect? in Wang, M. C., and Boyd,

W. L. (eds.), *Improving results for children and families: Linking collaborative services with school reform efforts* (Greenwich, Conn.: Information Age Publishing, 2000).

47. Ibid., 20; Council for Chief State Officers, *Family support, education and involvement: A guide for state action* (Washington, D.C.: Council for Chief State Officers, 1989).
48. Epstein, J., *School, family, and community partnerships: Preparing educators and improving schools* (Boulder: Westview Press, 2001).
49. Heir, T., Eliminating ableism in education, *Harvard Educational Review, 72, 1* (2002), 1–32.
50. U.S. Department of Education, *To assure the free appropriate public education of all children with disabilities: Twenty-third annual report to Congress on the implementation of the Individuals with Disabilities Education Act* (Washington, D.C.: U.S. Department of Education, 2001).
51. Refer to IDEA Final Regulations, 1997.
52. Singer, L. T., Arendt, R., Minnes, S., Farkas, K., Salvator, A., Kirchner, H. L., and Kliegman, R., Cognitive and motor outcomes of cocaine-exposed infants, *Journal of the American Medical Association, 287, 15* (2002), 1952–60.

Glossary of Related Terms

ADD (attention deficit disorder): A condition classified as a medical diagnosis by the American Psychiatric Association's *Diagnostic and Statistical Manual of Mental Disorders.* Individuals are diagnosed as having ADD based on their inability to concentrate and, in some cases, on their impulsiveness and hyperactivity. Almost 10 percent of school-age children are thought to have this disorder. Some children, according to IDEA regulations, can qualify for special education services based on having this disorder. Those who suffer from attention deficit disorder and also are hyperactive are diagnosed with ADHD (attention deficit hyperactivity disorder).

Aid to Families with Dependent Children (AFDC): Started back in the 1930s, AFDC programs were designed to provide cash grants to families with children in the United States and U.S. territories whose incomes are not adequate to meet their basic needs. Families are also eligible for AFDC support if they have a child who is financially needy due to death, incapacity, or parental abuse. This program is slowly being phased out and replaced with the Temporary Aid to Needy Families Act of 1996.

American Civil Liberties Union (ACLU): An organization with the primary mission of defending and preserving the individual rights and liberties guaranteed to all Americans by the Constitution and laws of the United States.

Bayley Scales of Infant Development: A test that measures mental, physical, social, and emotional development. The scales are normed after children from ages one month to forty-two months, and use four scales: motor quality, attention and arousal, emotional regulation, and orientation and engagement.

Center for Reproductive Law and Policy (CRLP): A nonprofit organization started in 1992 by a team of lawyers and activists to protect the laws and policies that guarantee reproductive rights and other freedoms to women.

Cocaine: A derivative of the coca plant. Cocaine can be used three different ways: inhaled through the nose in powder form, in injected in liquid form, and smoked. The drug acts as a powerful central nervous system stimulant and a local anesthetic. Cocaine constricts blood vessels, causing a rise in blood pressure and an increase in heart rate. An overdose can result in sudden cardiac arrest and even death.

Coke users: People who used cocaine when the drug became popular during the 1970s. Often considered glamorous, they were frequently in the entertainment field and other upper-class circles.

Crack: A smokable and highly potent form of cocaine. It is a nearly pure form of cocaine that is heated, soaked, and cut with an agent. Crack cocaine hardens into a lump of rock with the texture of porcelain. When the substance is smoked, it produces a crackling sound, thus the name crack. In less than ten seconds it leads to a state of euphoria that lasts less than fifteen minutes.

Crack abusers: Crack abusers, often poor inner-city residents, used crack, the cheaper form of cocaine, during the drug epidemic of the 1980s. Unlike coke users, who tended to have a higher socioeconomic status, crack abusers were socially constructed as criminals who tore apart urban neighborhoods to support their habit.

Crack baby: A baby who was prenatally exposed to crack.

Crack mother: A term coined by the media, referring to urban women who used crack during pregnancy.

Early childhood special educators: Teachers who work with young children who are at risk for early school failure or who have developmental disabilities.

Early intervention: An educational program that is designed to give children a jump start before they enter school. Such programs target children from traditionally disadvantaged backgrounds for educational interventions. These programs also provide training in areas such as nutrition and parenting skills for the caregivers of children participating in the program.

Emotional and behavioral disorders: Disorders, including schizophrenia, characterized by consistently aggressive, impulsive, or withdrawn behavior. Each state classifies these conditions differently. Children are generally classified as having an EBD if their behavior impairs their personal, social, academic, and vocational skills.

Family preservation programs: In 1993 Congress passed legislation for the establishment of Title IV, Part B of the Social Security Act, which created funding for family preservation programs. These support programs were built around the theory that families that are about to have children placed in foster care would be more amenable to receiving services and learning new behaviors.

Fine motor skills: Involve the development of the small muscles used in the movement of fingers and in hand-eye coordination. The development of fine motor skills is encouraged by the maturation of the central nervous system, and plays a key role in the cultivation of intelligence.

Foster care: Home placements for children whose parents are unable to care for them due to abuse or neglect. Caregivers in foster homes range from unrelated adults to grandparents and other biological relatives.

Full inclusion: A principle according to which all students, regardless of handicap, are placed in a regular education classroom or program on a full-time basis. All services must still be provided to the child while in that setting.

Great Society programs: Federal programs started in 1964 under the Johnson administration to alleviate poverty, reduce hunger and malnutrition, expand health care, provide better housing to low-income families, and make the poor more employable.

Gross motor skills: Functions required in order to control large muscle movements, such as walking running, sitting, or crawling.

Inclusion: The commitment to educate each disabled child to the maximum extent appropriate in the school or classroom the child would attend if not disabled. It involves bringing the support services to the child, rather than moving the child to the services, and requires that the child benefit from being in the class, as opposed to having to keep up with the other students.

Individuals with Disabilities in Education Act (IDEA): A landmark 1975 federal law, originally known as the Education for All Handicapped Children Act. Under this law, in exchange for federal funds, schools must guarantee all children with disabilities a "free and appropriate" education. The law has been amended several times to include services for children from birth to age twenty-one.

Infants and toddlers: Children under the age of three years.

Longitudinal study: Research in which data is collected on the same group of individuals at intervals over a period of time. Studies in which information is collected once a year using different groups of people are cross-sectional, not longitudinal.

Mainstreaming: The selective placement of special education students in one or more regular classes. This term refers to the IDEA's preference for the education of all children in the least restrictive environment possible, in which children with disabilities are educated in classrooms alongside without disabilities whenever possible.

Polydrug use: When a drug abuser takes a combination of substances, such as marijuana, alcohol, tobacco, and other illicit street drugs.

Postnatal risk factors: Things that contribute to adverse developmental outcomes of children after they are born, such as chaotic lifestyles, unstable home environments, poverty, malnutrition, violence, and postnatal exposure to drugs.

Prenatal care: Routine health care provided to women during pregnancy. A health care provider monitors the mother and fetus and provides information to and treatment guarantee the best possible outcome.

Prenatal drug exposure: Refers to the exposure of the fetus to cocaine, alone or in combination of other substances, during pregnancy.

Preschool-age children: Children between the ages of 3 and 4 years.

School-age children: Children age 5- and up. Children are considered school-age when they enter kindergarten.

Special education: Educational programs designed to serve children with mental and physical disabilities. Special education children are entitled to interventions ranging from speech therapy to mathematics tutoring. Traditionally, special education students were taught in separate classrooms. Increasingly, more children are being offered special education services in regular classrooms with their peers.

Stanford-Binet Intelligence Scale: A standardized test that assesses intelligence and cognitive abilities in children. The scale is also used as a school placement tool to detect the presence of learning disabilities or developmental delay and in tracking intellectual development. In addition, this test is used in neuropsychological testing to assess the brain function of individuals with neurological impairments.

Veteran teachers: Teachers participating in the study with twenty or more years of experience.

Index

Pennsylvania, 12
Personal Responsibility and Work Opportunity Reconciliation Act, 11
poor, the, 7; biases against, 12; children, 107; families, 105; sterilization of, 18; stimatization of, 16; undeserving, 7–8
poverty: addiction and, 10, 19, 76, 105, 114; drug-abusing women living in, 18, 105; drug-exposed children and, 62, 105, 114; early intervention and, 93; solutions to, 7; urban, 60
Powell, Diane, 104
prenatal care, 140; drug treatment and, 9, 14, 90–91, 96–97; drug-abusing pregnant women and, 18, 23, 25–27, 30–31; effects of, 28; maternal health and, 90
prenatal drug abuse (*see also* drug-abusing pregnant women): alcohol, 24, 25, 28 (*see also* alcohol); Black women and, 6, 8; criminalization of, xv, xvii, 8, 15; developmental issues and, 22–23, 39; effects of, 30–32, 44; heroin, 24; hospital testing for, 8, 11, 32, 60, 64; in urban areas, 59–61; Latina women and, 8; marijuana, 24, 25, 28; media framing of, xvii, 4–6; polysubstance, 24, 25, 27, 28; poor urban women and, xvii, 3, 24; preventing, 90–91; research on, 30–32, 53; severity of, 30–31; social construction of, 5; social policy and, 89; tobacco, 24, 25, 28; treatment for, 9, 14, 89, 90–91, 96–97; White women and, 5–6, 8
prenatal drug exposure, xvi, xvii, xviii, 8, 17, 140; addressing, 19, 89; assessing, 64, 101, 102; child welfare policy and, 8; developmental issues of, xviii, 21, 22–23, 30, 39, 81, 106; early intervention and, 39, 89; epidemiology of, 81–82, 106–107; human services policies and, 4; impact of, 3, 5, 28, 88; inner city, 62; longitudinal studies of, 87, 128n. 26; long-term effects of, 4, 30; misunderstanding, 64–66, 100; preventing, 90; risk factors associated with, 30, 67; traditional early childhood disablitity and, 38
preschool education programs: for drug-exposed children, 95–97
Problem Behavior Scale (PROBS 14), 33
Project DAISY (*see also* Washington, D.C.), 48, 103–104; school interventions and, 103
Project Prevention (*see also* C.R.A.C.K.), 15; sterilization of drug abusers and, 16

public assistance. *See* social welfare
public education: early school failure and, xvi; policy issues and drug-affected children, 53, 58, 84, 89–90, 112–14
public health: drug addiction and, 19, 90; initiatives, 40; policy, 91
public hospitals: drug testing in, 8, 11, 60, 64
Public Law: 104–193 (Personal Responsibility and Work Opportunity Reconciliation Act), 11; 105–17, 39; 105–89 (Adoption and Safe Families Act), 13; 96–272 (Adoption Assistance and Child Welfare Act of 1980). *See* Public Law 105–89
public school reform: at-risk children and, 112–14; educational policy and, 112–14; full inclusion and, 73; funding for, 107–108, 114; interventions and, 112
public school system: expanding definition of drug-exposed children by, 75–80; limited resources of, xvii, 114; response to drug-impacted children by, 58, 80–83, 98–99, 100, 102–12
public schools: communities and, 90, 107; drug education programs in, 81, 108; drug-impacted families and, 105; health and social services within, 113–14; identifying drug-exposed children in, 63–71, 98–100; in poor neighborhoods, 81; interagency collaborations and, 105–106; interventions in, 81, 98, 100, 102–12; learner diversity and, 113; parental involvement in, 113; social support systems in, 76, 98, 105–106, 108, 113; social workers in, 76, 79, 105–106, 107; urban, xii, 63, 80, 88, 108, 113; violence in, 81
punitive policies, 11; Black and Latina women and, 8–10

R
Ravenswood City School District: Parent-Child Intervention Program (PCIP), 48
Reagan adminstration, 7
Reagan, Ronald, 7
Reeves, J. L. and R. Campbell, 6
Republicans, 7
responsive classroom model: drug-exposed children and, 102–107, 112
Richardson, G. A., 29